Deirdre K

CW00571534

RAGING

Three Plays/
Seven Years of Warfare in Ireland

Wild Sky: The Rising

Embargo: The War of Independence

Outrage: The Civil War

NICK HERN BOOKS

London

www.nickhernbooks.co.uk

Fishamble: The New Play Company presents

OUTRAGE

by Deirdre Kinahan

Outrage was first produced by Fishamble: The New Play Company, in partnership with Dublin Port Company, and Meath County Council, during St Patrick's Festival, as part of the Department of Tourism, Culture, Arts, Gaeltacht, Sport and Media's Decade of Centenaries programme. It was commissioned by Meath County Council Arts Office, and ran in the Kells Courthouse and Pumphouse in Dublin Port from 17 March–3 April and then was streamed online.

Cast

PJ	Naoise Dunbar
Alice	Caitríona Ennis
Nell	Mary Murray

Creative Team

Playwright	Deirdre Kinahan
Director	Jim Culleton
Set Designer	Maree Kearns
Costume Designer	Catherine Fay
Lighting Designer	Kevin Smith
Composer & Sound Designer	Carl Kennedy
Hair & Make-up	Val Sherlock
Dramaturg	Gavin Kostick

Production Team

Producer	Eva Scanlan
Production Manager	Eoin Kilkenny
Associate Producer	Cally Shine
Stage Manager	Sophie Flynn
Assistant Stage Manager	Síle Mahon
Wardrobe Supervisor	Aoife O'Rourke
Technical Venue Manager	Laura Murphy
Chief LX	Matt Burke
Production Coordinator	Ronan Carey
Marketing	Dafni Zarkadi and Freya Gillespie
FOH Coordinator	Daniel Culleton
PR	O'Doherty Communications
Music Advisor	Gerardette Bailey
Original Song by	Michael Brunnock
Set Construction	Andrew Clancy
Cover Artwork by	Leo Byrne and Publicis Dublin
Filmed by	Media Coop

Dublin Port Company

Port Heritage Director	Lar Joye
Head of Special Projects	Jim Kelleher
Dublin Port PMO	Colin Hartford

Meath County Council

Arts Officer	Gerardette Bailey
Librarian	Ciarán Mangan

The production runs for approximately 75 minutes, with no interval.

Songs in the production are:

'Ochón, Caoineadh Airt Uí Laoghaire' – from *Grief* by Eithne Ni Uallacháin & Dónal O'Connor

'Siúil A Rún' – traditional

'Róisín Dubh' – traditional

'Take it Down from the Mast' – James Ryan 1923

'Bonfire of the Vanities' – Michael Brunnock 2022

An education pack to accompany this production is available for teachers on request. Please contact **info@fishamble.com** for details.

About Fishamble

Fishamble is an Irish theatre company that discovers, develops and produces new plays of national importance with a global reach. It has toured its productions to audiences throughout Ireland, and to 19 other countries. It champions the role of the playwright, typically supporting over 50% of the writers of all new plays produced on the island of Ireland each year. Fishamble has received many awards in Ireland and internationally, including an Olivier Award.

'the much-loved Fishamble [is] a global brand with international theatrical presence... an unswerving force for new writing'
Irish Times

'Ireland's leading new writing company' **The Stage**

'the respected Dublin company...forward-thinking Fishamble'
New York Times

'excellent Fishamble...Ireland's terrific Fishamble' **Guardian**

'when Fishamble is [in New York], you've got to go'
Time Out New York

'that great Irish new writing company, Fishamble'
Lyn Gardner, Stage Door

'Fishamble puts electricity into the National Grid of dreams'
Sebastian Barry

Fishamble Staff: Jim Culleton (Artistic Director & CEO), Eva Scanlan (Executive Director), Gavin Kostick (Literary Manager), Ronan Carey (Office & Production Coordinator), Freya Gillespie (Fundraising & Development Executive), Cally Shine (Associate Producer), Dafni Zarkadi (Marketing Officer)

Fishamble Board: Peter Finnegan, John McGrane, Louise Molloy, Doireann Ní Bhriain (Chair), Ronan Nulty, John O'Donnell, Siobhan O'Leary (Vice Chair), Colleen Savage

Fishamble is funded by the Arts Council, Dublin City Council, and Culture Ireland.

Fishamble's recent and current productions include

- *The Treaty* by Colin Murphy (2021–22) in Ireland, Irish Embassy in London, and online as part of the Decade of Centenaries and Seoda Festival

- *Duck Duck Goose* by Caitríona Daly (2021–22) touring in Ireland, and online

- *On Blueberry Hill* by Sebastian Barry (since 2017) touring in Ireland, Europe, Off-Broadway, West End, and online

- *Before* by Pat Kinevane (since 2018) touring in Ireland, internationally, and online, as well as a bilingual version *Before/Sula*

- *Mustard* by Eva O'Connor (since 2020) on tour in Ireland, internationally, and online

- *On the Horizon* in association with Dirty Protest, by Shannon Yee, Hefin Robinson, Michael Patrick, Oisín Kearney, Samantha O'Rourke, Ciara Elizabeth Smyth, Connor Allen (2021) online

- *Tiny Plays for a Brighter Future* by Niall Murphy, Signe Lury, Eva-Jane Gaffney (2021) online

- *Embargo* by Deirdre Kinahan (2020) online during Dublin Theatre Festival

- *Tiny Plays 24/7* by Lora Hartin, Maria Popovic, Ciara Elizabeth Smyth, Caitríona Daly, Conor Hanratty, Julia Marks, Patrick O'Laoghaire, Eric O'Brien, Grace Lobo, Ryan Murphy (2020) online

- *The Alternative* by Oisín Kearney and Michael Patrick (2019) on tour to Pavilion Theatre, Draíocht, Belltable, Everyman Theatre, Town Hall Theatre, and Lyric Theatre

- *Haughey | Gregory* by Colin Murphy (2018–19) in the Abbey Theatre, Mountjoy Prison, Dáil Éireann, Croke Park, and Larkin Community College, as well as on national tour

- *The Humours of Bandon* by Margaret McAuliffe (2017–19) touring in Ireland, UK, US, and Australia

- *Rathmines Road* by Deirdre Kinahan (2018) in coproduction with the Abbey Theatre

- *Drip Feed* by Karen Cogan (2018) in coproduction with Soho Theatre, touring in Ireland and UK

- *GPO 1818* by Colin Murphy (2018) to mark the bicentenary of the GPO

- *Maz & Bricks* by Eva O'Connor (2017–18) on national and international tour

- *Forgotten, Silent and Underneath* by Pat Kinevane (since 2007, 2011 and 2014, respectively) touring in Ireland, UK, Europe, US, Australia, New Zealand, and online

- *Charolais* by Noni Stapleton (2017) in New York

- *Inside the GPO* by Colin Murphy (2016) performed in the GPO during Easter

- *Tiny Plays for Ireland and America* by 26 writers (2016) at the Kennedy Center, Washington DC, and Irish Arts Center, New York, as part of Ireland 100

- *Mainstream* by Rosaleen McDonagh (2016) in coproduction with Project Arts Centre

- *Invitation to a Journey* by David Bolger, Deirdre Gribbin and Gavin Kostick (2016) in coproduction with CoisCeim, Crash Ensemble and Galway International Arts Festival

- *Little Thing, Big Thing* by Donal O'Kelly (2014–16) touring in Ireland, UK, Europe, US and Australia

- *Swing* by Steve Blount, Peter Daly, Gavin Kostick and Janet Moran (2014–16) touring in Ireland, UK, Europe, US, Australia and New Zealand

- *Spinning* by Deirdre Kinahan (2014) at Dublin Theatre Festival

- *The Wheelchair on My Face* by Sonya Kelly (2013–14) touring in Ireland, UK, Europe and US.

Fishamble wishes to thank the following Friends of Fishamble & Corporate Members for their invaluable support:

Alan & Rosemary Ashe, ATM Accounting Services, Mary Banotti, Tania Banotti, Doireann Ní Bhriain, Colette and Barry Breen, Sean Brett, John Butler, Elizabeth Carroll, Breda Cashe, Barry Cassidy, Maura Connolly, Finola Earley, John & Yvonne Healy, Alison Howard, Stephen Lambert, Damian Lane, Angus Laverty, Patrick Lonergan, Sheelagh Malin, John McGrane, Monica McInerney, Ger McNaughton, Anne McQuillan, Liz Morrin, Pat Moylan, Liz Nugent, Ronan Nulty, Lisney, Siobhan O'Beirne, Tom O'Connor Consultant, Siobhan O'Leary, Muiris O'Reilly, Andrew and Delyth Parkes, Margaret Rogers, David & Veronica Rowe, Judy Regan, Jennifer Russell, Eileen Ryan, Colleen Savage, Brian Singleton, William J. Smith, and Mary Stephenson. Thank you also to all those who do not wish to be credited.

fishamble.com   facebook.com/fishamble   twitter.com/fishamble

Acknowledgements

Thanks to the following for their help with this production: David Parnell, Liz Meaney, Elaine Connolly, Hannah Gordis, and all at the Arts Council; Ray Yeates, Sinéad Connolly, Brendan Teeling, and all at Dublin City Council Arts Office; Christine Sisk, Ciaran Walsh, Valerie Behan, and all at Culture Ireland; Eamonn O'Reilly, Lar Joye, Jim Kelleher, Colin Hartford, and all at Dublin Port Company; Gerardette Bailey, Ciarán Mangan, Vivian Hoey, and all at Meath County Council CUT Arts Office; Conor Falvey, Sinéad Copeland, Rónán Whelan, Orlaith Lochrin, and all at the Department of Tourism, Culture, Arts, Gaeltacht, Sport and Media; Ronan Nulty, James Kelleher, Karen Muckian, and all at Publicis Dublin; Matt Smyth; all at 3 Great Denmark Street; Michael Brunnock; Aisling O'Brien; Myles Dungan; Ger Gaughran & Hinterland Festival; The Bookmarket Café; Mark Smith, Carol Lee & Jass Foley of Sawmills Studios/KPW.

Biographies

Deirdre Kinahan is an award-winning playwright and a member of Aosdána, Ireland's elected body of outstanding artists. Recent work includes *The Visit* (Draiocht, Dublin Theatre Festival 2021); *The Saviour* (Landmark Productions 2021); *Embargo* (Fishamble 2020*); In the Middle of the Fields* (Solas Nua DC 2021); *Dear Ireland* (Abbey Theatre 2020); *The Bloodied Field* (Abbey Theatre 2020); *The Unmanageable Sisters* (Abbey Theatre 2018/19); *Rathmines Road* (Fishamble 2018); *Crossings* (Pentabus UK 2018); *Wild Notes* (Solas Nua DC 2018); *Renewed* (Old Vic London 2018). New projects include *OUTRAGE* (Irish Civil War Commemoration Play, Fishamble & Meath County Council), a new play for Landmark Productions, a new play for the Abbey Theatre, a new opera. Deirdre is an Associate Artist with Meath County Council Arts Office and artist in residence at CCI Paris November 21. Her plays are translated into many languages, published by Nick Hern Books, and produced regularly in Ireland and on the International stage.

Jim Culleton is the Artistic Director of Fishamble: The New Play Company, for which he has directed productions on tour throughout Ireland, UK, Europe, Australia, New Zealand, Canada and the US. His productions for Fishamble have won Olivier, The Stage, Scotsman Fringe First, and Irish Times Best Director awards. Jim has also directed for Audible, the Abbey, the Gaiety, the Belgrade, 7:84 Scotland, Project, Amharclann de hÍde, Tinderbox, The Passion Machine, the Ark, Second Age, Dundee Rep, Draíocht, CoisCéim/Crash Ensemble/GIAF, RTÉ Radio 1, Frontline Defenders, Amnesty International, Little Museum of Dublin, Fighting Words, RTÉ lyric fm, Soho Theatre, Scripts Festival, Baptiste Programme, Vessel and APA (Australia); TNL (Canada); Solas Nua and Kennedy Center (Washington DC); Odyssey (LA); Origin, Irish Arts Center, New Dramatists, and 59E59 (Off-Broadway); as well as for Trafalgar Theatre Productions on the West End, and IAC/Symphony Space on Broadway. Jim has taught for NYU, NUI, GSA, Uversity, The Lir, Villanova, Notre Dame, UM, UMD, JNU, and TCD.

Naoise Dunbar graduated from The Lir Academy in 2020. Recent theatre credits include *Duck Duck Goose* (Fishamble); *The Great Hunger, Fourteen Voices From The Bloodied Field* (Understudy, Abbey Theatre); *Wexford Playwrights Studio Readings* (Wexford Arts Centre*); As You Like It, Anatomy Of A Suicide, Merchant of Venice, Blood Wedding* (The Lir Academy). Film: *Lakelands* (Harp Media); *Tara* (Short).

Caitríona Ennis has performed in *Mabel's Magnificent Flying Machine* (one woman show, Gate Theatre, Dublin); *Duck Duck Goose* (Fishamble); *14 Voices from the Bloodied Field* (Abbey Theatre); *Dear Ireland* (Abbey Theatre); *The Fall of the Second Republic* (Abbey Theatre); *A Christmas Carol* (The Gate Theatre); *Country Girls* (Abbey Theatre's touring production); *Cuckoo* (Soho Theatre, London); *Ulysses* (Abbey Theatre); *Porcelain* (Peacock/Abbey); *A Holy Show* (Peacock Theatre); *Dublin by Lamplight* (Corn Exchange, Abbey Theatre). *Test Dummy,* nominated for Best Actress in the Irish Times Theatre Awards

2016 (WeGetHighOnThis in association with Theatre Upstairs); *The Table* (Performance Corporation in association with Boca Del Lupo, Magnetic North Festival in Vancouver); *Wild Sky* (Irish Arts Centre New York, and an Irish national tour); *Scuttlers* (Royal Exchange Theatre Manchester); *Spinning* (nominated for Best Supporting Actress in the Irish Times Theatre Awards 2015, Fishamble: The New Play Company); *Sluts* (Edinburgh Fringe 2011); *The Lark* (Smock Alley Theatre); *Narf* (Smock Alley Theatre); *Annabelle Star* (The Ark); *A Whistle in the Dark* (winner ISDA Award for Best Actress 2011); *A Couple of Poor Polish Speaking Romanians* (nominated for Best Actress, ISDA 2010). Caitriona has performed with ANU Productions, directed by Louise Lowe in *The State Commemoration, Taking to the Bed, The Boys of Foley Street* (nominated for Best Actress in the Irish Times Theatre Awards 2012); *Thirteen (*nominated for Best Actress at the Dublin Fringe Awards 2013); and *Angel Meadow* (winner of MTA Best Over All Production and Best Ensemble, HOME Manchester).

Mary Murray toured extensively with Fishamble in *The Pride of Parnell Street, Noah and the Tower Flower* and *Tiny Plays for America and Ireland* and she's delighted to be working with them again. Her stage performances have taken her to China, Europe and the United States and she's picked up Best Actress and Supporting Actress awards with MAMCA, 1st Irish Theatre Festival in New York and The Irish Times. On screen she's best known for playing Janet in *Love/Hate*. Other notable productions include *Valhalla, The Wonder, Penny Dreadful, Adam and Paul, The Magdalene Sisters, Dead Still* and *Let the Wrong One In*. Mary is the director of www.visionsdrama.com You can find out more about her on her website Facebook or YouTube. @marmurray

Maree Kearns is a set and costume designer based in Ireland. She is a frequent collaborator with Fishamble having previously designed *The Alternative, Rathmines Road, Invitation to a Journey* and *Maz and Bricks*. She has designed sets and costumes for many of Ireland's other leading theatre companies including The Abbey Theatre, Anu Productions, CoisCeim Dance Theatre, Verdant Productions, The Cork Opera House and The Corn Exchange among others. Maree is also the course director for the MFA in Stage Design at the Lir Academy in Dublin.

Catherine Fay designs for theatre, opera and dance. She has designed *The Treaty* and *Embargo* for Fishamble: The New Play Company. Her most recent work is *Portia Coughlan* (Abbey Theatre); *iGirl* (Abbey Theatre); *Elektra* (Irish National Opera); *Walls and Windows* (Abbey Theatre); 14 Voices (Abbey Theatre); *Transmission* (Little Wolf) for DFF 2020; *Much Ado about Nothing* (Rough Magic Theatre Company); *Näher... nearer, closer, sooner* (Liz Roche Dance Company); *The Return of Ulysses* (Opera Collective Ireland); and *The Plough and the Stars* (Lyric Hammersmith/Abbey). She designed *Girl Song* (United Fall); *12 Minute Dances, Totems* (Liz Roche Dance Company); *Owen Wingrave* (Opera Collective Ireland); *Acis and Galatea* (Opera Theatre Company); *The Importance of Nothing* (Pan Pan Theatre Company) and *Owen Wingrave* (Opera Bastille, Paris, 2016). She has designed many productions for The Abbey Theatre including *The Plough and the Stars* (Irish Times Theatre Award nomination 2017); *Our Few and Evil Days* (Irish Times Theatre Award nomination 2015); *Henry IV Part I* (Irish Times/ESB Theatre Award nomination 2007). For The Gate, she has designed *Romeo and Juliet* (Irish Times Theatre Award nomination 2016) and *The Threepenny Opera*. Other work includes *Breaking Dad* (Landmark Productions, Irish Times Theatre Award nomination 2015); and *Dogs* (Emma Martin Dance, Winner Best Production and Best Design for ABSOLUT Fringe Festival 2012).

Kevin Smith trained at The Samuel Beckett Centre, Trinity College Dublin. This is the fourth time he has a designed a Deidre Kinahan premiere, having previously designed *Spinning* with Fishamble, *These Halcyon Days* with Tall Tales & Landmark Productions which won a Fringe First in Edinburgh and *Wild Sky* with Ten42 Productions. His other theatre-design credits include *Class with Inis*, Abbey Theatre which recently won a Fringe First in Edinburgh. Also *Monsters Dinosaurs & Ghosts* (Abbey Theatre, Peacock Stage); *Rhinoceros* (Blue Raincoat Theatre Co); *Scenes from the Big Picture*, *In The Next Room*, *Three Winters*, *La Ronde* (The Lir); *Barney Carey Gets His Wings* (Barnstorm); *Beowulf The Blockbuster* (Pat Moylan Productions); *The Family Hoffmann Mystery Palace* (The MAC & Cahoots NI); *Driving Miss Daisy*, *Moll* (Gaiety); *The Faerie Thorn*, *Puckoon* (Big Telly). His dance design credits include *12 Minute Dances* (Liz Roche Co.); *Coppelia* (Ballet Ireland); *Manefesto* (Maiden Voyage). He also designed *An Outside Understanding* with Croí Glan which was nominated for Best Design Absolute Fringe). Kevin's opera-design credits *include Vampirella, Saints & Sinners and Clori Tirsi é Fileno* with RIAM and *Flatpack* (Ulysses Opera) which was nominated for an Irish Times Best Opera Production.

Carl Kennedy has worked on numerous theatre productions, working with venues and companies including Fishamble: The New Play Company, The Gaiety, The Abbey, The Gate, Rough Magic, Landmark, Decadent, The Lyric Theatre, Theatre Lovett, ANU Productions, HOME Manchester, Prime Cut Productions, HotForTheatre, Speckintime, Gúna Nua and Peer to Peer among others. He has been nominated three times for the Irish Times Theatre Award for Best Sound Design. He also composes music and sound design for radio, TV and video games. He was composer and sound designer *for Mr Wall* on RTÉJr which was shortlisted for an IMRO Radio Award in the 2018 drama category. Game titles include *Curious George, Curious about Shapes and Colors, Jelly Jumble, Too Many Teddies, Dino Dog* and *Leonardo and His Cat*. TV credits include sound design for *16 letters* (Independent Pictures/RTÉ) and SFX editing and foley recording for *Centenary* (RTÉ).

Eoin Kilkenny has toured across Ireland and the world with theatre productions from Landmark Productions, Rough Magic Theatre Company, Fishamble: The New Play Company, CoisCéim Dance, Abbey Theatre, and many more. He has worked at some of the best festivals at the Traverse Theatre, Edinburgh, during the Festival Fringe, Galway International Arts Festival, Melbourne International Arts Festival, Dublin Fringe Festival and London international Festival of

Theatre. He trained as a production manager with the Rough Magic SEEDs programme, working on their productions in Dublin, Belfast and New York. He is a product of UCD Dramsoc and has completed an MA in Producing at The Royal Central School of Speech and Drama.

Sophie Flynn's stage-managing credits include *The First Child, Medicine, Grief Is The Thing With Feathers, Happy Days, Postcards from the Ledge, Arlington, Once, Ballyturk, Breaking Dad, Talk of The Town, The Second Violinist* (Landmark); *Three Short Comedies, The Seagull, Druid Gregory, Cherry Orchard, The Beacon, Epiphany, Richard III, King of the Castle, Beauty Queen of Leenane* (Druid); *Translations* (National Theatre); *The Field* (Lane Productions); *The Heiress, Who's Afraid of Virginia Woolf?, Pride and Prejudice, An Ideal Husband, The Threepenny Opera, Enemy of The People, Krapp's Last Tape* (The Gate Theatre); *Trad, The Dead School* (Livin Dred). Her film and television credits include *Gilgamesh* (Macnas); *St Patrick's Day Parade '19, Dancing With The Stars* (Shinawil); *Play Next Door* (VIP); *Lunasa* (RTÉ); *Obama Concert, College Green* (MCD); *Magners League Awards, Vodafone GAA Awards, Take Me Out, The Childline Concert, IFTA Awards* (Observe); *Deal or no Deal* (Endemol Productions); *The All Ireland Talent Show* (Tyrone Productions).

Síle Mahon is a graduate of The Lir National Academy of Dramatic Art where she studied a BA in Stage Management and Technical Theatre for 3 years. Her most recent work includes Assistant Stage Manager on *The Treaty* with Fishamble: The New Play Company; Stage Manager on *Man Down* with Róisín Whelan Dance and Costume Assistant on *The Book of Names* with ANU Productions. She has also worked on many theatre productions in her time in The Lir Academy. Her work in training involves: Stage Manager on *Midwinter, Julius Caesar* and *As You Like It*; Assistant Stage Manager on *Summerfolk* and *Salome, or the Cult of the Clitoris: A Historical Phallusy*; Costume Supervisor on *The Unreturning* and Chief LX on *Anatomy of a Suicide*.

Eva Scanlan is the Executive Director at Fishamble: The New Play Company. Current and recent producing work includes *Outrage* by Deirdre Kinahan; *The Treaty* by Colin Murphy and *Embargo* by Deirdre Kinahan, both as part of the Decade of Centenaries; *The Alternative* by Michael Patrick and Oisín Kearney; *On Blueberry Hill* by Sebastian Barry on the West End, Off-Broadway, and on Irish and international tour; Fishamble's award-winning plays by Pat Kinevane *Before, Silent, Underneath* and *Forgotten* on tour in Ireland and internationally; *The Humours of Bandon* by Margaret McAuliffe; *Maz and Bricks* by Eva O'Connor; *Inside the GPO* by Colin Murphy; *Tiny Plays for Ireland and America* at the Kennedy Centre in Washington DC and the Irish Arts Centre in New York; and *Swing* by Steve Blount, Peter Daly, Gavin Kostick and Janet Moran on tour in Ireland, the UK, and Australia. Eva produces *The 24 Hour Plays: Dublin* at the Abbey Theatre in Ireland (2012–present), in association with the 24 Hour Play Company, New York as a fundraiser for Dublin Youth Theatre. She has worked on *The 24 Hour Plays* on Broadway and *The 24 Hour Musicals* at the Gramercy Theatre in New York. Previously, she was Producer of terraNOVA Collective in New York (2012–2015), where she produced *Underland* by

Ally Collier; *terraNOVA Rx: Four Plays in Rep* at IRT Theater; the soloNOVA Arts Festival; the Groundworks New Play Series; *Woman of Leisure and Panic* (FringeNYC); *P.S. Jones and the Frozen City* by Rob Askins, among other projects. She has worked on events and conferences at the New School, the Park Avenue Armory, and Madison Square Garden.

Cally Shine has worked across the United States as an actor, teaching artist, company manager and creative producer. Born and raised in Seattle, WA, she holds a BA in Theatre and a Minor in Irish Studies from the University of Montana and a Graduate Diploma in Cultural Policy and Arts Management from University College Dublin. When not working with Fishamble, Cally is an Assistant Producer at Once Off Productions.

Gavin Kostick works with new writers for theatre through a variety of courses, script-development workshops and award-winning schemes as Literary Manager at Fishamble. Gavin is also an award-winning playwright. His works have been produced nationally and internationally. Favourite works for Fishamble include *The Ash Fire*, *The Flesh Addicts* and *The End of The Road*. Works for other companies include *This is What We Sang* for Kabosh, *Fight Night*, *The Games People Play* and *At the Ford* for RISE Productions and *Gym Swim Party* with Danielle Galligan in co-production with The O'Reilly Theatre. He wrote the libretto for the opera *The Alma Fetish* composed by Raymond Deane, performed at the National Concert Hall. As a performer he performed *Joseph Conrad's Heart of Darkness: Complete*, a six-hour show for Absolut Fringe, Dublin Theatre Festival and The London Festival of Literature at the Southbank. He has recently completed a new version of *The Odyssey*, supported by Kilkenny Arts Festival.

RAGING

Three Plays/Seven Years of Warfare in Ireland

Wild Sky: The Rising
Embargo: The War of Independence
Outrage: The Civil War

Introduction
Deirdre Kinahan

Three plays; seven years of warfare in Ireland; and my own fifty-three years of fascination with the bloody birth of our nation.

I grew up in the shadow of one of the major players in the 1916 revolution, Padraig Pearse. I used to play in the grounds of his mother's house, racing across the fields and climbing the bizarre follies that dot the parklands of what was his extraordinarily progressive Gaelic school at the turn of the century: St Enda's, Rathfarnham. I literally lived ten minutes' walk from his home. I used to cycle along the stony paths through the woods of the grounds, play roly-poly on the small hill next to the old classrooms, peer in the window at the old desks and dusters, wondering 'What was it all like back then?' I was always one for 'What was it all like back then?'! When my young friends wanted to play Red Rover or rounders, I might suggest a game of Henry VIII killing all his wives, or Anne Devlin refusing to rat out Robert Emmet when captured in Kilmainham Jail. The centuries always disappeared for me, and the stories grew and grew in my imagination. So to have a voice in Ireland's commemoration of her revolution is honestly one of the greatest privileges and the greatest thrills of my writing career.

I was, however, initially wary of the 'history' play. It is a tricky beast. It can be didactic, overloaded with information or worse still... boring! So when Meath County Council asked me to write a play inspired by the events of the 1916 Easter Rising I was both delighted and a little nervous. Considering every Irish household has a story of brutal murder, deliberate starvation by local English landlords, or Granny hiding guns in her knickers to keep them safe from British soldiers, I wondered how Irish households might react to the actual truth of the period.

Similarly, there is the tragic reality of continued warfare in Northern Ireland; a rump state created in the midst of that time;

and then, of course, Ireland's strong culture of celebrity historians, professional historians, amateur historians, extremely vocal historians who might take great offence at the free imaginings of a playwright dancing on their turf! But I have always believed one has to put fear in one's pocket when writing anything for public consumption so off I danced, sporting for a good old jig with Ireland's ghosts.

***

Wild Sky was the first play – and where I learned how to tackle history in my own way. The play is pure fiction, but like all art it grows out of real human experience, human passion, human story. It is my attempt to turn back the clock, to walk the roads, to feel the heat, and dream the dreams that brought about Easter 1916. It is a play about radicalisation, what draws the young to revolution, what brings about the scream for change. Written through the prism of three ordinary, young, rural Irish poor, it is as much a love story as it is a comment on the time, and for me an homage to the very real ideals that took root having blown in from troubled Europe on Ireland's 'wild sky'.

The title comes from a poem by another neighbour, this time in my adopted county of Meath, Francis Ledwidge – poet, volunteer, amateur actor, socialist, lover, road-builder and republican – who inexplicably joined the British Army despite his nationalist credentials, only to be blown apart in the Battle of Passchendaele in 1917 during the First World War. Ledwidge wrote the poem for his good friend, teacher and playwright Thomas MacDonagh, one of the Irish leaders executed with Padraig Pearse after 1916.

He shall not hear the bittern cry
In the wild sky, where he is lain,
Nor voices of the sweeter birds,
Above the wailing of the rain...

The story of Francis Ledwidge became the bedrock of Mikey's experience in my play, and the story of another local woman, Kathleen McKenna, inspired the character of Josie. A neighbour told me in a chat: 'There was a fella apparently from out your way that fought in the GPO and then walked home, the whole way home, and was never arrested, just went back to his farm

like it all never happened and spoke very little about it.' And
that 'fella' became Tom Farrell.

***

The second play *Embargo* came about through a different route.
It was commissioned by Dublin Port, Irish Rail and Fishamble
Theatre Company who wanted to highlight the role of civil
militancy during the Irish War of Independence against Britain
– in particular the little-known national strike initiated by
dockers and train drivers, who refused to handle munitions or
transport British soldiers for a period during 1920–21, at the
risk of losing their jobs or worse.

It was a strike I knew little or nothing about myself, and
researching it brought me into the fantastic world of Irish
socialism and her burgeoning labour movement at the turn of
the century. I remember I was aghast to read about the various
soviets declared throughout the country during that period and
other great national strikes in 1918, '19 and '20, where vast
swathes of the population downed tools and took to the streets.
I was particularly enamoured by some of the slogans of the time
like that painted on a red flag over Knocklong Soviet Creamery
in County Limerick: 'We make butter not profits!' Why were
these stories so hard to find? Why were they not part of the
popular narrative surrounding our revolution?

I met a railman and historian, Peter Rigney, who took me into
the archives of Irish Rail and there I tried to piece together a
sense of the rail strike, and more generally a sense of the rail
world at that time and how crucial it was to British governance
and administration in Ireland. It was there that I also came
across a short article telling the story of a train driver who
refused to participate in the strike and so was tarred and
feathered by the Irish Revolutionary Army – but still drove his
train. I couldn't get over the image: a man tarred and feathered
but still roaring through the countryside in his steaming cab,
still raging.

Embargo grew entirely out of that image, because to me it
spoke so eloquently to the confusion, the mucky blur of
political allegiance, personal circumstance, and the horrific
violence of war, all war. Once again, I began to conceive of

three characters who could embody the forces, passions and conflicting truths of that time. Gracie, fresh from the trenches with a penchant for ladies' fabrics, is an unlikely hero, but he saves the fervent labour advocate Jane from her ultimate demise, thus drawing the ire of the traditional Irish revolutionary Jack.

The Irish War of Independence raged on for three years from 1919 to 1921. A genuine 'David and Goliath' story, where a deeply repressed population took on the might of one of the world's greatest empires and brought it to a point of truce. It was – and is – a most extraordinary feat. An extraordinary moment of defiance, of sacrifice, of ingenious battle and justified rage. But it came at a cost, an immense personal cost not only to the flying columns of young, armed, revolutionary men whose deeds are well documented, but also to legions of Irish citizens who played their part, who won and lost, who watched their homes and villages burn, their children die and their future form from the carnage of war.

Tragically what emerged from this glorious fight was not the egalitarian, Gaelic, progressive republic declared to an empty street by Pearse in 1916, but a deeply conservative, guilt-ridden, poverty-stricken Catholic caliphate that limped on into the 1920s after a brutal civil war.

***

Outrage, the third play in this volume, was another commission from Meath County Council, produced by Fishamble, with support from Dublin Port and the Arts Council. The play is the story of two sisters, Alice and Nell, who are deeply engaged and viscerally active throughout the entire period of revolution, and yet find themselves at a crossroads when the country descends into faction and civil war implodes. For me, this play is about narrative, about how history is always written by the victors, and inevitably by men. I found it fascinating when researching the role of women in Ireland's revolution that many of them worked in the realm of propaganda – writing war bulletins, pamphlets, leaflets, slogans – yet now, one hundred years on, their contribution is widely unrecognised and unknown. Women fought at the very heart of the movement from the get-go and they weren't simply making sandwiches or rolling bandages; they participated fully in every aspect of the Irish wars. Éamon de Valera, one of the leaders of 1916 and a major Irish political figure right into the 1970s, famously lamented that women were the most 'unmanageable' of all Ireland's revolutionaries, which one might put down to the fact that women had the most to fight for. The right to vote. The right to education. The right to work. To walk the streets. To some small smidgeon of personal independence, agency or joy.

Outrage grew out of the true testimony of three revolutionary Irish women, Mary Flannery Woods (mostly known as Molly), Brigid (Bridie) O'Mullane and Kathleen McKenna. It also revolves around an event which took place in 1923 in Kerry, where two women who supported the anti-treaty faction were violently assaulted by Irish Free State soldiers, refuting the notion that rape and sexual assault did not play a part in the Irish wars. Like *Wild Sky* and *Embargo*, the play focuses on the grassroot experience, on 'What was it all like back then?' for the ordinary citizen trying to negotiate a life in the heat of momentous change.

The Irish Revolution is to my mind, a great event, a necessary event, the event which sparked the fire and paved the way to Ireland's future – to the prosperous, progressive, European nation we eventually became. Like all nations, however, Ireland has her ghosts. Ghosts of revolution. Ghosts of love. Ghosts of hate. Ghosts of compromise. Their story is our story. Their story lives on in the heart of us. I will always be thankful for the opportunity as a playwright to give them shape, to give them voice.

***

I would like to acknowledge and thank all the brilliant creatives who have worked with me on these three plays: directors Jo Mangan, Maisie Lee and Jim Culleton; the magnificent actors, some of whom took part in more than one production; and the superbly talented designers, producers and other supportive personnel. None of this can happen without your magic.

Particular thanks are due to Gerardette Bailey, whose extraordinary vision brings such joy to arts and audiences in County Meath.

WILD SKY

The Rising (1916)

*Dedicated to the memory
of one of the wildest,
Karen Louw*

Wild Sky was commissioned by Meath County Council Arts Office, and first performed on 19 February 2016 at Rosnaree House, Slane. The cast was as follows:

JOSIE DUNNE	Caitríona Ennis
TOM FARRELL	Ian Toner
MUSIC PERFORMER	Mary Murray

Director	Jo Mangan
Lighting Designer	Kevin Smith
Costume and Set Designer	Niamh Lunny
Music Selected and Arranged by	Susan McKeown
Producers	David Teevan, Ten42 Productions in association with Meath County Council Arts Office
County Arts Officer	Gerardette Bailey
PR	Dairne O'Sullivan

The production was supported by Meath County Council; Department of Environment, Heritage & Local Government; 1916/2016 Centenary Programme and Culture Ireland.

Characters

TOM FARRELL, *eighteen*
JOSIE DUNNE, *seventeen*

This play is a site-specific piece with minimal set and lighting, to be mixed and underscored with music and traditional songs from the period.

Commissioned by Meath County Council Arts Office.

Poetic Quotes Woven into Text

Wild Sky (title) from 'Lament for Thomas MacDonagh' by Francis Ledwidge
1. From W.B. Yeats 'Prayer for My Daughter'
2. From W.B. Yeats 'Easter, 1916'
3. From W.B. Yeats 'Easter, 1916'
4. From W.B. Yeats 'Easter, 1916'
5. From Thomas MacDonagh 'A Dream of Hell'

TOM FARRELL. I wonder might she have come with me to New York. If I had asked her. If things had turned out different.

And I know it's daft, but sometimes I ask her now, after all these months, in my head, in my dreams. The way that I know that I should have. If I'd had the courage.

There were days before I left Slane that I thought that I saw her, was sure that I saw her. Through the window of Macken's... or on that turn to her house on the road. But it was always just a glimpse... a notion... not the full picture... it'd be just a hint of Josie, the bend of her elbow... the tilt of her head... the swirl of her feet.
I'd be sure though.
Sure!
In those days of endless waiting... after the Rising.
After the endless executions.
That it was Josie. It had to be Josie... before she'd vanish again on me... blown away on the wind.

Pause.

Mother used to throw stones at the wind on a gusty day. For fear that it was fuelled by fairies travelling from place to place and the chance that they might steal one of us from the crib. Curious how that came to my mind just as the order 'NOW' lurched forward from inside the choking flames of the GPO.
I was supposed to run but my feet stuck fast... stuck fast to the concrete like they might have had it been a rain-drenched bog. 'RUN, Tom, for fuck's sake, run' urged the boys at my side and heaved me out of my stupor... heaved me out of that doorway... but into what? I could see no enemy... I could see nothing... no more than my mother and her fairies. My eyes were so swollen in my head by smoke and heat... heat like I can hardly describe... heat that threatened to melt the gun in my hand, the air in my lungs, the skin on my back.

But instinct told me they were there… Soldiers, British
soldiers… and instinct told me not to dither once their bullets
rained.

There were thirty of us ran with The O'Rahilly as I've heard
since. Thirty fled the GPO in one swoop. Like swallows.
We led the retreat from their guns.
To Henry Street.
To Moore Street.
But sadly led no further.

I'll never know how I wasn't killed or how I found that nook.
The mind had stopped. The world had stilled. The sound of
gun and roar and death. It was in my heart and in my knees
as I danced like a man demented. Danced over the cobbles,
over the sparks of flying bullets and over the corpses that fell
before me. 'Dancing to a frenzied drum.'[1]
Then over that wall… to land… where?
In 'quiet'.
A quiet yard.
An open door.
I scurried on. A rat now. No more a dancer. No more a
soldier. Was I ever a soldier?
No time to think. I just saved it all up. Saved it all up in
pictures. Saved it up for Josie.

JOSIE DUNNE. Annie Hennessey, the schoolteacher from
Kilberry came to the Healy house to give step-dancing
classes of a Sunday evening. She came over on her bicycle,
a sinful way for any woman to travel according to the priest
but Annie Hennessey paid no heed.

Me, Tom Farrell and Mike Lowrey were let go to the classes.
Mrs Healy had no children of her own you see and loved
Mikey on account of his writing poems.
Mrs Healy was a grand woman but no dancer. I'll tell you
I could barely look at her some Sundays for laughing at her
leaping and general melee – she was too big really for the size
of her little feet and like a duck you'd be afraid she might
topple as she cracked ankles and lumped across the floor.
Mikey and Tom would sometimes waddle in behind her
kicking out their feet and waggling their arses in mockery.

I remember loving those evenings and the splendour of it all.
I'm telling you Healy's parlour was quite a sight to behold for
Slane. She had the very best of everything! And quite the lady
in the village, Mrs Healy was, friends with all the gentry
around. But still she couldn't contain her SCREAMING
enthusiasm for all things Gaelic so might have had twenty of
us up of a Sunday. And we all tap-tapping and bounding about
in circles to the screech of old McGoona's fiddle.
I remember one night Mr Healy burst in in a tizzy warning
that the very walls of the house would collapse if we didn't
stop our clod-hopping and incessant banging.

God... it all seemed such fun in the beginning.

TOM FARRELL. I was sweating and heaving now on a
flagstone floor. What was it? – A small kitchen. Dead now.
No fire in the range. A troubled chair. They must have fled.
My heart was bursting in my chest so I tried to slow it...
slow it and breathe easy. I was alone. The bullets too had
slowed outside. Nervously I lay my hands about me... 'Take
it easy, Tom'... 'Legs?', 'Belly?', 'Head?'... No holes!
I hadn't a scratch! 'God help us, Annie Hennessy, but I put
your jigs to good use that day.'

Afraid to stand for snipers, I dragged myself out into the hall
and up the quiet stairs. The Commandants in the GPO had
had us burrowing for days so I thought if I could get into the
attic perhaps I could move on down the houses and away
home... Home!?... Jesus.

Bedlam suddenly broke out again in the lane... a stream of
gunshot. I knew it must be another wave of our lads retreating
to the streets. Running fast. Running from the shaking walls,
the flaming roof, the blinding stench of carbon, carcass and
raging timber. Running ducks now for the soldiers, the British
soldiers, picking them off from the barricades.
How many were dead?
Christ.
Could there be anyone left at all?

I picked my way through the litter of lives abandoned to
those eaves. Not much to see – a chamber pot, abandoned
trunk, discarded well-worn boots, some crates, a broken doll.

Nothing to bar the way. Nothing like the stubborn granite we clawed at in the GPO with hammer and pick. Mad men, dreaming! Dreaming of what? Escape? But what was there to escape to for desperate men, desperate men in Dublin?
More hunger.
More lock-outs.
Dead babies.
Consumptive wives.
The degradation of the docks?
These were men like I'd never seen before – their stories like none I'd ever heard before – Men poorer than the poor of the fields – Dirt poor – Dogged poor – Dangerous poor – Nothing to lose – Pure – The pure men of the citizen army.

Should I let myself down now onto the landing?
Was it safe?
I listened.
'Minute by minute'.[2]
Nothing.
Should I wait?
Should I sleep?
I hadn't slept in days. Five days.
Had we lasted five days?... A week?... It was hard to tell now. The world was altered, nothing sure, not even time... not even the sun... the revolving sun... I hadn't seen it for days... all I'd seen were faces... their faces... 'vivid faces'[3]... scorched then drenched... smiling... screaming... orders barked... a whirl of skirts as women came with tea and bandages through the smoke.
And some took up their guns and shot and killed and dug like the rest of us telling any man that objected to read his precious proclamation: '*Equal rights and equal opportunities to all its citizens.*' That's the whole people of Ireland, mister. Men, women and children!
Josie would have loved those women.
Josie...
I slept.

JOSIE DUNNE. Not to be outdone by the Gaelic Leaguers in Old Castle, Mrs Healy started her own drama group here in the village hall. It was great craic altogether, a mess of paint and flags and screaming. And every streel with a gob on him drafted in to carry a pick or beat a drum.

Our first play was *Cathleen Ni Houlihan* with yours truly playing the forlorn Delia Cahel.

JOSIE *is performing a piece from the play* Cathleen Ni Houlihan, *she has great fun playing all the parts but pointing to herself to let us know that she plays Delia.*

It starts with Peter... I'll play Peter... I'll play them all to give you an idea. Right. So. Peter...

PETER. There are ships in the bay; the French are landing at Killala!

DELIA. Michael! (*He takes no notice!*) Michael, why do you look at me like a stranger?!

PATRICK. The boys are all hurrying down the hillside to join the French.

DELIA. Michael won't be going to join the French.

BRIGIT. Tell him not to go, Peter.

PETER. It's no use he doesn't hear a word we're saying.

BRIGIT. Try and coax him over to the fire, Delia.

DELIA. Michael, Michael, you won't leave me! You won't join the French, and we going to be married!

She puts her arms about him, he turns towards her as if about to yield.

OLD WOMAN'S VOICE. They shall be speaking forever. The people shall hear them forever.

JOSIE *ends with a flourish.*

JOSIE DUNNE. It wasn't much of a part, Delia, in fact that's the best bit there I just played for ya. Wasn't much of an auld play if I'm honest! But everyone in the hall cheered and you couldn't get a seat and Mrs Healy said I was a natural!

Mikey was mad on Yeats but I'd have liked a bit more to say and I don't know why it's always the lads get to go off and fight... I think they just write the best parts for themselves.

Anyway we moved to our new cottage in December that same year, 1913. And it's a grand house altogether, with an acre. And just across the road from Mike Lowrey's! We got it just after Daddy died and thank God for that because there was room now for Grandad who could help me keep an eye on the little ones with Mammy off to work on Healy's farm. Not one of us had to be put into the industrial school because I left my own studies and took up a job in Macken's and between that and Mammy's shillings we could make do. McGoona was raging all the same. He told Grandad he'd his eye on me for teaching and complained that all his best scholars had to leave to be maids or miners or shop girls.

But I loved the shop. I did. I loved it. All the smells. Of ham or bread or roasted coffee beans. And the material in the draper's – Silk! Real silk! And soft wool. And taffeta. And all sorts I wouldn't know the name of but loved to rub my hand over if Mrs Macken needed assistance at that end of the shop. It was a busy enterprise, fierce busy and Mr Macken was delighted with me because I caught onto everything quick.

But the best of all was where it was situated! Bang slap in the middle of the village where you could see everything. Sure you'd see every stranger or neighbour that came up the street and it was always easy to get a message to me or for the little ones to come in for a sweet after school.

I'd see Mikey heading off every morning to the copper mines where he got work.
And then Tom would nod through the window as he walked with his father toward the field with the cattle.
I'd see Father Clavin heave up the hill on his bike for the afternoon tea and poetry readings at Healy's. Growing fat as a fool he was on cake and Gaelic.
And then Lord Dunsaney!
Or Headford!
In a splendid motor car.
Or those recruitment men when they started! A scourge to the county they were, knocking on doors and tormenting all the young fellas to go off and join the army... the British Army!... To go off and fight in the war!

'Whose war?' asked Annie Hennessy.

And wasn't she right.

Sure it had nothing to do with Ireland.

'It was the English', she said. 'And the Germans. And a host of others squabbling over Empire!' Empire! When we were lucky to have a roof over our head.

'Why should we care about poor little Belgium,' she'd say 'when we don't have any freedom of our own?'

She was some woman Annie Hennessy. I'm telling you, she knew it all. And she'd argue as well as any of them. Her and Mikey were always at it. She wouldn't agree with him you see that Home Rule would come in for Ireland after the English war. She said it was a trick. She said Carson and the Ulster volunteers would see us all in hell first. And sure the English loved Carson, no matter what they promised, they'd only play us all for fools.

They'd go at it after every meeting – Annie and Mike. But then they'd be as thick as thieves at the same time so I was more than a little uneasy I can tell you, until Mikey finally kissed ME after that dance in Donaghmore.

And I never felt anything like it.

Sure I thought I'd drown in sheer pleasure of it.

The wet, soft, steaming pleasure of it.

And I'd waited SO long.

SO long.

Since school!

Since way back!

With him always walking me home or walking me here or walking me there and never anything else!

I'll tell you I thought I'd go crazy because I knew Mike Lowrey could have any girl he wanted. In Slane. Or Drogheda even. Or anywhere-abouts with those eyes and his fine back and his poems and his constant blather!

I was always stone cracked about Mike Lowrey!

TOM FARRELL. I fell in love with Josie Dunne when I was six years old. Though I knew I'd never have her. Josie Dunne sat at the top of our class. She was a raging beauty and master of every task put before her. She could sing like an angel and calculate at speed and knew as much about Finn McCool and

them Celtic heroes as old McGoona with his book and his
chalk. I knew every hair on her head and every twist in her
face as she laughed, cried, taunted or danced as we made our
way to school.

Herself and Mike Lowrey were the real scholars though...
I was just a pretender, *Mike's pal*. I got into Mrs Healy's
house because Mike asked me. I got into the drama group
because Mike needed lads to paint the scenes. I got into the
Volunteer Army because Mike founded our own group of
Hurley-Bandits here in Slane. I got into all sorts without a
thought just to be close to Josie Dunne. Just to hear her pitch
and plot with Mikey and the rest of them. The real dreamers.
The real thinkers. The real rebels.

I wouldn't hear a word she said sometimes. Locked in the
roll of her small pink tongue, round lips, or flash of a
smile... the words were just 'meaningless words'[4]. It was the
tilt of her head alone that would leave me spinning. Josie
Dunne had a mole, dark as earth, just below her left ear. You
wouldn't see it unless you knew her because she fought with
her hair to conceal it. But I knew it and I loved it. I watched
it break free into the light sometimes if she threw her head
back to laugh or sing or if she turned quickly to see who was
coming. And I imagined licking it, kissing it, stroking it,
from the thatch of her hair to the small of her back. That
mole was mine. My door to Josie Dunne. Dark and
abandoned. Only mine.

In the village they began to say she was trouble – too much
cavorting with Annie Hennessy. And her Grandad Pat was a
known Fenian, fierce for the stories and supporter of patriots,
land agitators, cattle drivers and conspirators. Though his
back was long broke with rheumatism he could still talk
politics, Home Rule and treason with a cast of characters like
Brian O'Higgins.
O'Higgans! A fanatical poet that cycled the length and
breadth of Meath knocking Irish into a dose of dunderheads
like me put before him by the Gaelic League. We fell foul of
his teaching once a week but stuck it out because Mrs Healy
would serve lemonade to anyone who could say their name
in Irish.

Tomás O Fearrail!
Ferocious he was... So can you imagine my surprise when
I came across him on the roof of the GPO... still roaring!
But a sight more dangerous now with a gun in his hand.

My mother tried to warn me off Josie Dunne and the
Volunteers and the Gaelic League. 'It's only auld blather'
she'd say 'And what use is it? Isn't it the same Irish they
beat into you that was beaten out of us twenty years ago?...
Stay well away, Tom, and keep your eyes on New York. Your
brother nearly has your passage saved.'
But I couldn't stay away.

JOSIE DUNNE. I dreamt one night I shot John Redmond.
Aimed my rifle high and took the head off the leader of
Ireland's Parliamentary Party – because he was the man who
always seemed to get in my way.

Annie Hennessey had long given up on Redmond because
she said he wouldn't have women in the Party but Mikey
thought he was God Almighty and so did Mrs Healy,
McGoona and the rest of them. Grandad of course was a
different story... he was a Fenian through and through and
he said the new IRB boys were the boys with the brains and
they knew what it would really take to get Home Rule. You
have to fight he'd say...'And fight on your own turf... not
off in France or Egypt for Christ's sake!'

Grandad ate the pamphlets and newspapers that Annie
brought back from Dublin... *The United Irishman, The
Citizen* even *Bean Na h'Èireann*! Grandad said that now was
the time to strike. He could feel it in his waters.
'England's difficulty is Ireland's opportunity! And there are
men and women (would ya believe it!) not afraid to do it!'

John Redmond only made him mad with his parliament and
his promises and his telling Irishmen to go fight in an
English war. 'Carson and Asquith are only making an eejit
out of Redmond,' he said. 'They want fodder for their guns.'
So there'd be killings when him and Mikey got to talking.
One night I had to actually throw Mikey out of the house for
fear Grandad would have a stroke... and the two of them
shouting and roaring the same worn arguments. But it all

raged round and round in MY head all the same – like squally rain. And I couldn't help but think there must be something else... another way to live. You see I'd get no time with the County Council or the Volunteers or The Board of Guardians or the Hibs or the IRB... because I wouldn't be let, I was just a woman, just a girl. Yet I looked to my mother. My beautiful mother, fit enough all right to do the work of a man in the fields, fit enough to keep house and home together, to feed the lot of us, to teach us and keep us out of harm's way. But she had a say in nothing – my mother. No one asked HER to vote for John Redmond or to throw him out. No one asked HER what was right for Ireland or Meath or Slane or her own front door! I saw my mother shed tears of useless grief for my father, tears of worry for me and my brothers and tears heavier than the clay from sheer exhaustion but still she was expected... WE were expected to bow our heads and SAY nothing... ASK nothing... HOPE for nothing. Just bow to the priest, to the Healys, to the lords and the judges, to John Redmond and the British... and to live... to live our lives bent double. Sure we knew no other way... 'til the day that Annie Hennessey took me up to Dublin! And there I met the Ladies of Inghinidhe na hÈireann and the Irish Women's Suffrage League. O God! What a day that was...

TOM FARRELL. There was a curious quiet about the house when I awoke. I peered down through the hatch. All was in darkness. I let myself down. There were two doors shut tight on the landing. I gripped my rifle and crept down the stairs not wanting to bring danger... but Jesus Christ what lay before me. A twisted crumpled mass of a woman... half her head blown off... and a thick pool of blood still rippling around her and into another room. I heard a door click on the landing and swung round with my rifle cocked just in time to catch two bloodshot eyes dripping out of the doorway: 'Don't shoot, you fool... you'll bring the Tommies in on top of us, haven't they already shot up half the street looking for yiz... get on with you why don't ya... haven't you bastards caused enough trouble.' And with that he shut the door.

I wanted to leave the house but in stepping over the woman's skirts didn't I skid in the slick of her blood and land on my arse on the floor. It was the mercy of God my gun didn't go off, because there, under a small scrubbed table, shivered a boy. We were face to face, his eyes like saucers in his skull. 'That's me ma,' he said, 'she wanted to go find Da and me brother but took a bullet through the window before she got to open the door.' I sat there speechless. What had I done? What was this all for? Why were women turned into corpses? Boys into orphans? Who the hell was shooting who and what was our grand plan?

My name it is Tom Farrell and I've a rifle in my hand. But my head's not full of Socialism or Eutopia or a Gaelic Republic... I have no convictions, no excuse. I'm only here because I love Josie Dunne... because I long for Josie Dunne. I've sleepwalked into history, guided by my groin and now I sit here amidst a dead woman's pots and pans with gunshot screaming round me and the entire city in flames. 'Do ya want a bon-bon?'
The boy held it out like it was the Eucharist. 'I've two left,' he said. Only then did I notice his nest. Sweet papers – hundreds of them. 'We emptied lemons on the Liffey,' he said, with his pals and his brothers the day the looting started. He lost a tooth on a liquorice and now his mother into the bargain.
We found a bit of a tablecloth in the table-drawer and covered up her head.
The house was divided into flats he told me but only him and old Divis that I'd met on the stairs were home. The others were lost somewhere, out there, in the mayhem. I could hardly make out his features with the tear-stains, snot and grime but I knew the look in his eyes. He'd be a citizen army boy if he were older... hardship, hunger... they were no strangers. We shared biscuits and water from my knapsack and waited... for what we didn't know.

JOSIE DUNNE. First we had lunch on Grafton Street at Bewley's Café amidst all the grand shops and toffs and hats and bustle. We met two of Annie's friends – actresses! – who worked sometimes in some place called The Abbey but also with Inghinidhe na hÉireann as teachers and campaigners for women's votes and better housing and children's treats and school meals, democratisation, the Irish language and a Women's Workers' Union! I'd never heard talk like this before... it was another world... and just beginning! Annie and I took part in their anti-recruitment walking! We started off at the Rotunda and walked in pairs down the length of Sackville Street passing out our leaflets to soldiers' sweethearts. The leaflets were written to remind them of their Irish patriotic duty and to have nothing to do with the British Army. We had to hide them in our muffs and distribute them quickly so as to get away before the soldiers saw their content. Helena, Annie's friend, warned me to be quick because some of the soldiers might take off their belts to try to beat us off the street! But what actually happened was that a policeman saw us and we had to take to our heels down Henry Street and Moore Street and away. The police couldn't catch us because of their heavy overcoats... I was thrilled and scared and astonished all at the same time.

These women talked about 'Ireland'. Ireland like it was a country all of its own. And women's votes. And women's jobs. And women's rights. And it all made sense. It just made sense. That Ireland could be different. And Ireland could be decent. And Ireland could be a place where everyone had a meal and a job and a home.

We took the train home, pink with excitement and told Tom Farrell all. Because Tom collected us in his cart. And Tom laughed at our adventure. And Tom told us we were two great women!
Tom Farrell never told you to be careful... or to be quiet... or to go easy because, I suppose, well, Tom Farrell never thought so much of himself so as to be telling other people how to live their lives.
Tom. He just... never got rattled or restless like the rest of us.

TOM FARRELL. It was dark again when the boom of the great gun to the North grew still. Pot shots were still sounding on the pavement, boots on the march... a motor turning.

JOSIE DUNNE. Our favourite place to walk was along the ramparts down by the Boyne – Me and Mikey. We would lie in a nest of long grass and look up at the sky... up at the birds, their free flight. Their swoops, their falls.

Mikey knew the name of every bird and every tree and every flower in Meath. He loved them all and he loved me as we clung and clutched and kissed and climbed...
Mike Lowrey left me breathless.

So how could he leave?

After all I'd told him.
After all our promises.
And with the English... the Fusiliers!
How could he...?
Choose Redmond over Ireland?
And Redmond over me?

TOM FARRELL. Some buildings moaned into collapse yet it seemed quieter... Dublin was quieter than before. I thought of Mikey. Where was he? Gallipoli? France? Belgium? What on earth would he make of all this? The fight. The week that was in it in Dublin, because he was the real rebel, Mike Lowrey, not me but he joined the wrong army. He followed Redmond's call, like thousands... thinking that if they fought for the British in France, they might give us our freedom at home but he, they were sold a pup... fed a lie... our independence would never be won in England's war and now he, they... all die on the wrong side.

JOSIE DUNNE. When Mike told me he was joining up to fight in France I screamed... and I'm sure they heard me up in Dublin and all along the road and through the ditches... because I knew... I knew as soon as he said it, it was the end.

TOM FARRELL. At first light I told the boy that I thought it was time to go. 'Good luck to you, bog-man,' came the whisper from under the table. 'Good luck yourself', said I.

JOSIE DUNNE. Mikey left his house on a bright Tuesday morning. I stood at our gate across the road with Mammy... and Grandad. 'A stillness strange crept'⁴ into my heart but still we wished him well. 'Don't worry, Josie, I'll be home soon... I love you.'

TOM FARRELL. I found a milk-cart overturned in the lane with a dead man under it. So I tossed my rifle without a thought and donned his cap and turned the cart toward Phibsborough.

In half an hour I was clear of the city... the ravaged bleeding city... gap-toothed, smouldering and furious... the remnants of our green quilt for a flag still fluttering over the carnage. The shawlie women and every rag-tag from the tenement now took back their streets. They hurled abuse and kicks and sticks at the bewildered survivors of the rising. *Sons of Éireann,* they were ridiculed now, lambasted for their pitiful revolution, for upsetting king and country... for spitting in the face of the sacrifice of other Irish husbands, brothers, fathers up to their neck in the muck and killing of Flanders.

I saw them marched away like ghosts... my comrades. Scorched now, limping now, exhausted, estranged, with heads down, tormented... scorned by the very people they fought to make free.

JOSIE DUNNE. I stood in the shop placing small green cards on every product we had that was Irish. It was a notion I'd got from the Dublin girls to promote Irish goods for Irish jobs but Mr Macken was having none of it. As he stood there glaring, urging me not to be drawing attention to myself I could feel the coughs again rattle up through me. My head was swimming and my chest was sore... Mr Macken looked alarmed.

But Grandad said the Dunnes were a hardy breed and I was happy to believe him. A spout in bed and I'd be right as rain and back behind the counter. It wasn't consumption. He was sure. There had never been consumption in our family.

Still, everyone stayed away.

Everyone, that is, except Tom Farrell. Or on the odd day Annie Hennessy.

Tom called every evening with news or sweets or flowers he'd pull out from the hedges. And Tom would sit right on the edge of my bed without a care. So I'd ask him if he'd heard from Mikey? I'd ask him if he'd heard anything from any of the lads that went over? I'd write letter after letter to Mikey in France. And Tom would post them for me down in the village. I was so afraid that Mikey was dead. That I might never have him again... feel him again... smell that gorgeous smell of man and musk and rain.

'God he was a fool to go, wasn't he, Tom?'
But Tom would only nod his head.
Always nodding.
No company at all.
His visits just died in the silence.

TOM FARRELL. I wanted to stop as soon as I saw them. The
Rebels. I wanted to take my place in their line, so I could feed
once more on youth, and courage and dreams. I wanted to run
from my own confusion. From the emptiness of my killing.
Because I never had their vision. Or Mikey's. Or Josie's.

JOSIE DUNNE. The blasted cough now seemed to shake the
very walls. And there was blood in it. Scarlet on the sheets.
Scarlet on my skin.

TOM FARRELL. I was born to the fields of Meath. I learned to
walk while planting seeds. Bred for emigration, I am pliable,
expendable, not worthy of the plough on my back... or...
OR can I make a man out of the digging – digging through to
Henry Street? Make a man out of the dragging? Dragging
explosives hither and thither avoiding sparks and flames that
might blow us all to bejaysus! Can I make a man out of the
singing, the shooting, the catching of a comrade as he falls to
the shock of a bullet.
Can I learn from them at all?
From Margaret Skinneder who says she'd as much right to
plant a bomb as any man and was willing to die while
trying?
From Josie Dunne who still believes in the chance of a
different world, a different life for all and sundry despite the
creeping choking death that steals up through her?
Can I?
Can I ever be worthy?

JOSIE DUNNE. Annie Hennessey was busy with preparations,
but for what she wouldn't say. She spent half the week in
Dublin making bandages and food hampers and first-aid kits
and she was always out on manoeuvres or at meetings or at
talks. O I wish... I wish to God that I was there with her. In
the thick of it... because 'it's coming', I hear her whisper to
Grandad, 'it's coming... and our boys are ready!'

Then I hear Macken call with a basket. Ham and bread and all sorts and a book of poems by Katherine Tynan. He's a kind man Mister Macken and it was hard to say what he had to say but he couldn't have people thinking that there was sickness in the shop and he couldn't have me handling all his apples and carrots and eggs. I was a fine girl, said Mister Macken, and he'd no doubt but that I'd recover but sure he had to think of business and wasn't it shocking the way the war was dragging on!

Dragging on!
I could barely drag myself now from my bed to the little window... the effort seemed to steal the air... but it was so nice when I got there. So nice to taste the cool breeze as it blew in from across the river... or to see the wild sky... our sky... And to imagine Mikey walking under it... on a battlefield or in a trench because they say they live in trenches out there in France, in holes in the ground... and they say they shoot out into the air, into nothingness, the same way that people here would sometimes throw a stone at the wind.

TOM FARRELL. My mind swam as I walked the roads home. Walked the roads home to Josie. And the roads knew nothing of the GPO or Bolands Mill or our fight in Dublin, the roads just turned and twisted in the same gentle generous way, through grasses and wild-flower and crop and the roads were silent – no echo of marching feet or rosary-bead or collapsing granite like I had left behind.

JOSIE DUNNE. Annie burst in the door last Monday... her face crimson purple! 'It's ON, Josie... it's started! 'What?' says I. 'They've taken over Dublin... Padraig Pearse and the Volunteers. It's all the news at Fairyhouse Races where they're trying to sober up the British soldiers to send them back to the city to fight! There's thousands of our lads out... well, hundreds! In Sackville Street and Stephen's Green and the women and all are with them so I'm going up on my bicycle to see what I can do. Mrs Healy's donated hams. Jesus, I'd put you on the saddle if you were able'... 'I'm able,' I cried, 'I'm able'.

It was nonsense of course. There wasn't an ounce of strength in me, I could get no further than the front door... and there

we found Tom Farrell coming in with a fist-full of
bluebells… the first ones out to be found. Annie flew off
down the hill at a pace, hair and hams flying. So I turned to
Tom and I begged him… to bring me to up Dublin… to take
a stand… a stand, Tom, for Ireland, for freedom, for self-
government, for your brothers and mother and mine. For
starving children, and dead fathers, for workers and for
Mikey because he'd never have gone, Tom. He never have
gone if he'd known this would happen, he'd never have gone
to the bloody war. But Tom just caught me up in his arms
and brought me back to my bed. I begged. Tom!
And then… of all things… he kissed me. He kissed me full
and forceful… right on the mouth – Tom Farrell! 'All right,
Josie, all right, I'll go,' and he was away up to Dublin… for
Ireland and for me.

TOM FARRELL. There was talk all right of a skirmish when I
made it as far as Ashbourne. Police had been killed at a hold-
up at Rath Cross but nothing more. No one asked me who I
was or where I was going. No one minded the state of my
clothes, the fright on my face or the scorched matt of my
hair. Their talk just turned to bullocks and calves and sheep
like it's turned for generations.
'Jesus,' I wondered, 'did the fight, my fight, our fight… did it
happen at all?'

JOSIE DUNNE. If I listened hard I could hear it, all the way from
Dublin – and down over the Boyne – the boom boom boom of
England's big gun. The one that blew Dublin to smithereens.
Grandad said that they sailed it in on the Liffey and now the
whole city was burning! I could see he was afraid now. Afraid
that when it was over… our lads would all be hung.

TOM FARRELL. Finally I could see it – the Boyne – as it
broke out free from the green and swung on into the valley.
It seemed to welcome me home.

JOSIE DUNNE. If I listened hard I could hear them. Through
the grasses. On the road. Different men now: Tom Farrell…
Mike Lowrey… walking home.

TOM FARRELL. And Slane Castle just as I left it! Proud gates,
strong and impregnable… like a mockery to me now and all
the dead of the week.

JOSIE DUNNE. If I listened hard I could hear them... pause at the top of the hill.

TOM FARRELL. I looked down toward Josie's cottage. And I collected all of the pictures, all of the people in my mind. For I would tell her every moment, every thought and every name.
I yelled the first one out to the wind,
Henry Coyle.
I saw him drop from a bullet on Moore Street.
Philip Clarke.
Husband, father, worker, born in the village of Slane.
Margaretta Keogh.
Citizen, Suffragette, Cumann na mBan.
I roared their names to the heavens.
Edward Ennis, Gerald Keogh, Francis Macken.
And sang them back to the heron.
Lizzy Kane, Louis Byrne, Patrick O'Connor.
Then I fired them at the castle walls.
Richard Murphy, Sean Owens, Michael Malone.
As I walked home. Home to where it all had started... with dancing and hurleys and loving Josie Dunne.

Where it all blew in on the wind... on the wild sky.

JOSIE DUNNE. If I listened hard I could hear them crying.
And Mammy...
I could hear her call the doctor.
Hear her call the priest.

TOM FARRELL. 'You were away,' said my mother as I bent back into the cottage. And I could see her hold tight to the milk jug for fear it might drop to the floor.
'I was,' I said.
'Then you'll not have heard will you... you'll not have heard about Josie Dunne.'

TOM *is stricken.*

Josie!
'She died only yesterday, son.
The consumption took her.'
Josie!

TOM *sits, shocked and silent. He is exactly as he was at the beginning of the play. He repeats his first lines.*

I wonder might she have come with me… to New York. If I had asked her. If things had turned out different…

End.

EMBARGO

The War of Independence (1920)

Dedicated to my great friend
Gerardette Bailey

Embargo was first produced by Fishamble: The New Play Company, in partnership with Dublin Port Company and Iarnród Éireann, as part of the Department of Tourism, Culture, Arts, Gaeltacht, Sport and Media's Decade of Centenaries programme. It was streamed live and on demand in October 2020, as part of Dublin Theatre Festival. The cast was as follows:

JACK	Callan Cummins
GRACIE	Matthew Malone
JANE	Mary Murray
Director	Maisie Lee
Set and Lighting Designer	Zia Bergin-Holly
Costume Designer	Catherine Fay
Composer and Sound Designer	Denis Clohessy
Hair and Make-up	Val Sherlock
Dramaturg	Gavin Kostick
Artistic Director of Fishamble	Jim Culleton
Producer	Eva Scanlan
Production Manager	Eoin Kilkenny
Line Producer	Cally Shine
Stage Manager	Steph Ryan
ASM	Sarah Purcell
Production Coordinator	Ronan Carey
Marketing	Chandrika Narayanan-Mohan
Wardrobe Supervisor	Cathy Connell
Dialect Coach	Gavin O'Donoghue
Chief LX	Gary Maguire
Lighting Crew	Suzie Cummins
	Cillian McNamara
Sound Operator	James Blake
Stage Crew	Vincent Doherty
	Hugh Roberts
	Damien Woods
Set Construction	Ger Clancy
Set Scenic	Eugenia Genunchi

Production Support	Production Services Ireland and One Louder Sound
Transport	Trevor Price Ltd
PR	O'Doherty Communications
Graphic Design	Publicis Dublin
Promotional Photography	Mattieu Chardon
Production Photography	Anthony Woods
Filmed by	Media Coop

Dublin Port Company

Port Heritage Director	Lar Joye
Head of Special Projects	Jim Kelleher
Dublin Port PMO	Colin Hartford

Iarnród Éireann

Events & PR Manager	Jane Cregan
Corporate Communications Officer	Hayley Durnin

Author's Note

In this play we are in no man's land. The characters are ghosts looking back at a moment in their shared history. We weave in and out of one fateful scene on a Dublin to Belfast train and hear three inner narratives as the characters remember, recreate and re-evaluate their role within this conflux of historical events.

The style is not realism, there are elements of direct address and chorus as the voices and stories cross and intertwine steaming on to the final moment of Gracie's flight. I see the three of them separate, no attempt at a realistic re-enactment of the scene on the train... they are storytelling.

The play can be performed anywhere. I don't see any props or set or furnishings. The characters build the pictures, then wipe them away before disappearing back into the walls of time. I do have a soundscape in my head, however, fading in and out... the sounds of the docklands, the train station, soldiers, city and perhaps some songs/music from the period could meander in?

D.K.

Characters

GRACIE, *male, twenty-six but looks older, originally from Cork but now living in Dublin working for the Great Northern Railway*

JANE, *female, thirty but looks older, from Dublin, she is a widow on the run from the police*

JACK, *male, seventeen, from Rathfarnham in Dublin, a member of the IRA and fireman on the train*

Note on Text

When lines are in bold there is an element of choral speaking as explained in the stage directions. At times all three characters speak together and at other times only one echoes the speaking character as marked.

Time

September 1920.

Setting

Amien Street Station, Dublin.

Commissioned by Fishamble Theatre Company.

GRACIE. My mother was a whore for the Greeks, not in the
    literal sense, no, not Helen of Troy like, she just loved their
    stories.
    And so my mother was all I could think of as that one-eyed
    fuck, Francis Deavy, thrust his fist into my mouth, stripped
    the shirt from off my back and pushed me face down into
    that wet Meath muck... a suffocating blend of shite and
    stone and water.
    'You are found to be a traitor to your country.
    'Let this be a warning to you and all other railway scabs.'
    And so it came, thick and fast, the hot black tar, burning
    down onto my head and back like lava.
    It took three of them to hold me down.
    And treat me to a shower of kicks, as the odious solution
    found home in every crease and every fold of my twisting
    carcass.
    And then the feathers.
    Like a sprinkling of caster sugar on a charred sponge, too
    lumpy and contorted to deserve it.
    White feathers.
    Like those that Daedalus fastened onto his son's wings.
    Their purpose was to shame... but thanks to the mammy and
    her Greeks I think it was those feathers that set me free.

    The mammy, you see, put great store into the lessons of
    Icarus and Medea and all them tortured creatures with their
    longings and betrayals, their divine copulations and violent
    ends. She'd hop home from the Carnegie Library after a full
    day working the markets, with a book under her shawl and
    the meagre makings of a dinner. Myself and the brother
    mopped up our gravy to tales of endless wandering, murder
    and raging kings. Not exactly standard fare for the teeming
    bare-footed residents of the Marsh, Cork City.
    The brother, who later found his Troy in the weekly
    broadsheet *An Claidheamh Soluis*, tried to bring her over to
    Cú Chulainn but the mammy decided that *Auld Cú* wasn't a

patch on the Greeks. She stuck to Achilles, Hercules, Odysseus and all them handsome if troubled foreign fellas.

And so it was her kind, wrinkled and smiling face that shot into my head that day as *the boys* treated me to their tar, their feathers and their savage humiliation. Mammy always said I flew too close to the sun and now I'd have the burns to prove it.

Rage is a curious event, isn't it?
An eruption so great that it might change the course of a life, just as lava might change the shape of a mountain.
And it was rage that gripped me in the aftermath of their IRA beating. When they tarred me. When they feathered.
And rage that granted me the strength to tear myself from off that post, snap the ropes they tied around me and march Spartan-like back into Kells railway station.

A woman appears, she has been running, she is desperate.

JANE. You've got to get me out of here, mister.

GRACIE *looks at her.*

GRACIE. But Kells is the end of my story.
I come here so I can go back to **the beginning**.

JANE. **The beginning.**

JANE *and* GRACIE *say this word together.*

JANE *then repeats her line exactly as she said it before.*

You've got to get me out of here, mister.

If you don't, they'll surely kill me!

They speak together.

That was how it started.

GRACIE. How my end started.
Just two days before the beating in Kells.
In the cab of the 10 a.m. Passenger and Goods.
Dublin to Belfast.

JANE. I jumped into the cab.
It was the 10 a.m. Passenger and Goods.

(*Together.*) **Dublin to Belfast.**
I was wild.
I was terrified.
The peelers were hot on my heels.
I had crossed. I knew. I had crossed some invisible line from sane, from safe, from struggle… to forsaken.
I knew. I knew I was in mortal peril now.
Because the truth is that I had straddled that line for most of my life… until that morning.
In those teetering times.
Revolutionary times.
Times of convulsion and danger.

JACK. I was due to fire the 10 a.m. Passenger and Goods.
Dublin to Belfast.

All three now say this line together, lines in bold from now on are spoken by all three unless otherwise indicated.

I was due to stoke the old engine up and see us off onto the coastal plains of North County Dublin. My favourite route on the Great Northern Railway where the spray of the sea would cool myself and the driver as we tore through our blessed and beautiful country.

I was only a few months on the job having abandoned my apprenticeship at Green's Apothecary much to my auld-fella's chagrin.
My auld-fella was a coward.
A mortification.
For he had turned his back on the war that was raging all round us, preaching pacifism, caution and sensible living instead from behind the safety of his grocery counter.
Howling out at the 'assassinations' and 'murders' being carried out by his fellow countrymen, burying his head in the bags of flour and tins of peaches or issuing warnings and lamentations from the top of his trembling newspaper.
My father.
I vowed I would never be like him.
I vowed I would never be a willing bond-slave to the British.
So I sought out the IRA as soon as I left school which was no trouble at all in Dublin.

My teacher out in Rathfarnham was a Master Fearraí. A Gealic League enthusiast, notorious for swaying off the usual course of study into intoxicating tales of Irish kings, Irish warriors, penal times, croppy boys, The Great Hunger, land wars, transported Fenians, the wounded Parnell, the brilliant O'Connell and of course our two beloved Pearse brothers murdered at Kilmainham in 1916 for their love of country. We were every one of us, as we walked into his classroom, revolutionaries in the making.

I got sworn in at sixteen like most of my childhood friends to the IRA Dublin Brigade 4th Batalion, by Séan Doyle. The very Séan Doyle that was shot in the back by the murderous British soldiers only a month before this **'beginning'** and he unarmed out on manoeuvres on Kilmashogue hill. But that there is a different story.

On the morning in question... this **morning**... I was walking the road from home to **Amiens Street Station**, when two of the boys tracked me down.
'Jack'... they said, 'We've news!'

The three of them now move into the scene of what took place that morning. They will slip in and out of this scene with ease as we proceed, tripping back into their own monologues, sometimes directly addressing the audience and sometimes echoing each other like a kind of chorus.

JANE. You've just got to get me out of here.

GRACIE. All right. All right, missus, what's the panic?

And with that she produced some class of a hook... blood... fresh dripping off of it.

Jesus, what have you there?

JANE. Never mind what it is... just drive the bloody train.

GRACIE. We're not due to leave 'til ten.

JANE. That's too late. Too late...

GRACIE. It's less than forty minutes off...

JANE. But they saw me... I'm sure of it...

GRACIE. Who saw you?

JANE. Please, mister, you've just got to get me out of here.

GRACIE. I will. I will.
   If you'll stop wielding that bloody thing.

JANE. I'm not afraid to use it.

GRACIE. I can see that...whose blood is it on it?

JANE. A bastard.
   A bastard's blood.
   I think I've killed the bastard...

GRACIE. Who?

JANE. It was at the back of the pump house... and I ran... and
   they seen me, I know they seen me.

GRACIE. Who?

JANE. The dockers.
   Some of the Nevin gang.
   And that's who Mick... who my husband used to work with.
   So they'll know where to go, they'll know where to send them.

GRACIE. Send who?

JANE. The polis of course... they'll go to our house on Moss
   Street... or surely folly me here.

GRACIE. The polis?

JANE. Isn't that what I just said!

GRACIE. All right... all right but... I need... will you please
   just put that thing down and then we will see what we can
   manage?

JANE. But why?... Why would I trust you?

GRACIE. And she locked her eyes onto mine.
   Dark black eyes.
   (JACK *says the line with* GRACIE.) **Like coals.**
   Lines of hurt and hardship carved deep beneath the lashes.

   Because I've no reason, no reason in the world to hurt you.
   And so we froze there.

For just a moment.
Trust, don't trust?
Scream, don't scream?
Kill or be killed?
And to think that I thought I had left the war behind.

JANE. I only wanted a job, a day's work for me brother Jimmy.
He was home from Liverpool with the work dried up.
Jimmy was a drinker but all I had after Mick died.
And he had a good heart, and he wanted to help.
He was me only hope.
To feed the kids.
And he'd been down to the docks for weeks now.
Trying to get a start.
Standing out on the Read in all weathers, hoping to get the
nod from Kiernan.
The bastard.
With his 'you, and you and you'.
Because that's what it was down the docks...
Kiernan and his like, gods on a thrust... holding the whole
cargo of work and the power to parcel it out every morning
to 'you and you and you'. There was nothing regular about
working the ships, nothing sure, you took your chances
every morning... competing with the next man for the
chance to lift your shovel.

He was a stevedore with no heart, Kiernan, and no
loyalty... the king of kickbacks and shillings left in
matchboxes and no one got a job on the north wall unless
they put a whiskey down for him in the pub the night before.

I knew Kiernan all my life.
He had an eye for me from the time I turned thirteen...
That's how I got my Mick his spot on the house-gang, with
regular work for years. Through Kiernan's eyes and
Kiernan's hands.
Thank God though Mick never knew it.
Mick wasn't from Dublin, wasn't from a docker's family so
he'd never have got a start if I didn't... I didn't give Kiernan
what he wanted.

Mick died.
My fine strong man.

His Achill lungs weren't made for Dublin.

His Achill lungs were made for the Atlantic mist not the choke and tar and violence of this city.

Dead, from shovelling coal from ship-hold to tub and tub to cart.

Dead, from sucking in the dust, the grain, the smoke and the potash for nigh on ten years.

Dead and soon forgotten as the docks swung back to the ships up for Palgraves, Carricks or George Bell.

All them hungry hands lifting hungry shovels.

But no one there to lift for me.

For me and mine.

I had to go down and try get a day's work for Jimmy.

So that we could eat...

And I knew Kiernan would be in the back bar of the Rail Hotel.

I knew he'd be in that small leather chair, sniffing his whiskey, counting his coins. Always there just before eleven.

So I put on a bit of rouge.

And I put on this blessed rag... my best dress.

And I went down the Rail Hotel.

And I opened the small back door.

And I stood there in the shadows.

Offering all I had.

All I had left to me.

If he'd just give Jimmy a start.

If he'd just give Jimmy a few days' work.

And so Kiernan follyed me out.

The bastard.

And on around to the Pump House.

Where he put one hand to me breast,

And the other to my throat,

Spittin' 'Tell me what makes ya think, when I've got me pick of all the young ones, that I would waste me cream, on a shattered old pig like you?'

And then he laughed.

Laughed.

Hard. Right into me face.

Rage is a curious event, isn't it?

An eruption so great that it might change the course of a life,

just as lava might change the shape of a mountain.
And it was **rage** that gripped me in the aftermath of
Kiernan's rejection. Kiernan's laughter. Kiernan's boot.
And **rage** that granted me the strength to snatch that docker's
hook from off the window ledge and tear it across Kiernan's
face, Kiernan's eyes and knock the bastard smack back onto
the cobble, before I ran lunatic-like out onto the Quay and up
here to **Amiens Street Station**.

She turns back to GRACIE.

So you see, mister. I have to get out of Dublin.

GRACIE. She had a pal, she said, up there in Belfast.
A pal that was like a sister to her.

JANE. She'll get me out.

GRACIE. They used to – (JANE *says this too.*) **work together
in Jacob's**.

JANE. We striked together. Marched together. Married together.
Dreamed and schemed and bore kids together. If I can get up
to Greta, she'll hide me, I know she will. She'll help. And
she'll get the kids up after. I know she will.

GRACIE. But are you sure you killed him?

JANE. There was blood bursting out from the back of his head
when he fell. I wasn't hanging around to find out, was I?
Please, mister, I can't afford to go to jail.
Not this time.
Not when I have four children.
They'll perish.
Please. I'm begging you.
Please get me up to Belfast.
Then I can make a plan.

GRACIE. All right. All right.
But put the bloody hook down, will you!
I'll have to square this with my fireman.
I don't know why he's late…
But sure you can squirrel in under there.
I'll get you as far as Belfast.

JANE. O God bless you.
God bless you, mister.

JACK. I had a skip in me step that morning.
I can still feel it, that skip we all had in **the beginning**.
After months of being out on manoeuvres.
Months of training.
Months of trekking over wild hills and vying for shot
practice.
Months of making and testing our tin-can explosives.
This was real. This was me finally doing something real.
My first strike for an Irish Republic.

GRACIE. She folded herself into a corner of the cab.
Crumpling with relief.
Silent now.
Still.
Save for the frayed – (JANE *says this too*.) **green ribbons**
of her bodice rising.
The only sign of life.

JANE (GRACIE *says this too*). **Green ribbons** for Greta's
wedding. I got that dress made by a tailor on Great Britain
Street. Such an extravagance and it only three months after
my own big day. It was early summer of 1913 and me and
Mick and Greta and Joe were all part of one big family, the
Union family. We all had work despite the strikes and Mick
and I had just set up in our own little house on Moss Street.
Just two families in that house and I after coming from a
tenement where there were nearly ninety of us swarming
about the place. Where I had little or no family, only the
kindness of me Uncle Jim. It was me Uncle Jim took me in
after my mother died, much to the annoyance of his own
wife, Nan, who had a growing brood of her own. So I never
felt like I belonged. Just an extra scrap on the scrapheap
foraging for food... or for a bit of love. I got to work early
I did. Dropping messages for the neighbours, delivering
parcels as a child or washing windows, washing steps. I even
worked for a time at the Rail Hotel, scrubbing vegetables,
scrubbing pots and carrying water through the kitchens.
That's where Kiernan spotted me first. He'd come in of a
morning after doling out the work on the docks. The thick

red head of him bending down over a small glass. I used to think he was a giant back then, the size of his great bulk squeezed into the leather chair in the back bar, where all **the carpet sellers and commercial travellers would dispense and display, brag and barter, swindle and sell**. And he had the ear of everyone, Kiernan, because he played friend to all men… **the bosses, the union, the workers, the polis, the shinners, the clergy, the volunteers, loyalists, socialists, parliamentarians**… he was a friend to all, because he believed in nothing, believed in no one, but himself. And he could appear out of nowhere… so silent for the size of him… with his rough hands and thick shadow and bristle sharp as a scrubbing brush. I used to dread him. I knew he wasn't a man you could say no to. Then Mrs Hardiman, the manageress got me a job in Jacob's and I got away from the docks, away from the Rail Hotel and I thought I was made. **Great days.**
Great days they were in Jacob's, when I met Greta and I met Mick and we fell in love and the three of us sang in the spring of our belief that we could change the world.

When Dublin was – (JACK *says this word too*.) **ablaze** with something new.
When – (JACK *says his name too*.) **Big Jim Larkin**'s fervent speeches had us all talkin' of workers' rights and workers' power… and agitation, emancipation.
(JACK *says this too*.) **And we could win!**
We could win that extra shilling.
Or we could win that fifty-hour week.
Dockers and drivers. Labourers and servants. **Bakers and postal workers.** Creamery men and seamstresses.
Together! (JACK *says this too*.) **We could win.**

And I believed. I really believed it all back then.
I was carried away on that wave of… hope. Yes, real hope that we could free ourselves from our pitiful existence with no say over our own governance or our own country.
Because we were united and we were family. And there was I in the thick of it. With the most tender of men holding my hand and the throat of us… like songbirds… calling for a better future. And the excitement of it. As we took to the

streets, with our banners and our badges and our youth.
There was such a sense of possibility. They were my days all
right, our days, great days –

JACK. Gracie –

JANE. Before the lock-out.

  JACK *arrives now onto the train.*

GRACIE. You're late.

JACK. I know but…

GRACIE. Where were you?

JACK. I'm trying to tell you. I got held up by a few of the boys.

GRACIE. What boys?

JACK. IRA. They got some information…

GRACIE. Well good for them… you, however, had best get
  shovelling or we'll never make ten o'clock.

JACK. What's this?

GRACIE. What's what?

JACK. Who's she?

GRACIE. She's… she's none of your business that's who she is.

JANE. I won't say a word.

GRACIE. She won't say a word.
  We're bringing her with us to Belfast.

JANE. I think it was the lock-out was the start of the hurt.
  Months we were out of work.
  Living on nothing.
  And I expecting my first baby…
  The lock-out was a stand-off like no other.
  And then Mick got hit by a polis down on Sackville Street
  during a riot. Bludgeoned he was to within an inch of his life.
  I'll never forget it… I was working on the press in Liberty
  Hall when one of the girls came running in, Jane! Jane!…
  they've killed Mick, they've gone and killed your Mick and

I ran… crazed, crazy to where she said he was but thank God
he was only knocked out, he wasn't dead but he was beat up
so bad that he could barely catch his breath. They had stood
on his chest, stomped and kicked, ribs broke, head split…
and he was never the same. He never had the same strength
after. But I was so grateful. So glad to have him back. To
have him alive and back in my arms to live out our **great
days**, great days when we were all still mad to be wearing –
(GRACIE *says this too*.) **green ribbons**.

GRACIE.…that were snatched and torn.
Lacklustre in their dying sheen.
Yet the urge to reach out and touch them still rose.
The urge to wrap my clumsy wrist around their regal tattered
softness. Or to place my face in a cushion of lace… get lost
in the heat of velvet.

JACK *returns to the scene and they all three play the next
few lines exactly as before…*

JACK. Who's she?

GRACIE. She's… she's none of your business that's who she
is.

JANE. I won't say a word.

GRACIE. She won't say a word.
We're bringing her with us to Belfast.

JACK. We're what?

GRACIE. Look don't you be concerning yourself, Jack. Just
pick up your shovel. We've to be off in twenty minutes.

GRACIE *returns to his monologue, he speaks to the
audience.*

I've always envied women their fabrics.
Not my poor mother's harsh wool but the cool of cotton on
younger girls or the precious silks such as you might see in
the shop windows of Cork.
It was ribbons got me through the war.
Ribbons and rouge and singing.
Hard to believe it now, but I was a pin-up.

Gracie Grace... the pride of the Munster Fusiliers.
I joined the British Army when I was seventeen.
Thinking I'd sail off to Greece with the Navy.
Come face to face with my mother's heroes.
But I was billeted in Tralee.
Given a short blast of training.
Then sent off to the bloody front!

I survived my first battle.
Festubert.
God only knows how, because I never lifted my head from
the mud and I never lifted my gun.
I wasn't cut out to be a soldier.
Not like my brother.
Not like Jason who fights now with this Irish Army.
Fights like a demon for an Irish Republic.
I... I put on concerts at the front.
I did!
Concerts!
So I could dance for king and country.
Sing for king and country.
In make-shift tents and depots and empty barns.
To provide some relief from the carnage.
There was a troupe of us.
A theatre troupe.
And our job was to mop up **death**.
To replace lost legs, lost brothers, lost minds... with singing.
To suture. To stitch. To pin up dreams of love and future and
happiness onto the bloodied walls of the trenches.
To side-step death with **illusion**.
Silence the big guns with music.
With play-acting. Or penny opera.
Magicians we were.
Conjuring up sweethearts and homesteads, turning ourselves
into jokers or kings or beautiful girls.
Our bollocks hidden away in the depths and folds of ribbons.

I think there is the potential for music to under play some of
GRACIE's memories and references to the war... echoes of
First World War songs like 'If You Were the Only Girl in the
World' or 'Mademoiselle from Armentières'. Just as a

soundscape of revolutionary fervour/oration/labour song can underlie some of JANE*'s speech above.*

JACK *returns to the scene.*

JACK. But we're not going anywhere!

GRACIE. What?

JANE. What?

JACK. That's what I've been trying to tell ya!
There's a horsebox full of soldiers to be brought up on this train.

GRACIE. What?

JACK. To Belfast!

GRACIE. No

JACK. The front hall is swarming with them.

GRACIE. Not when I came in?

JACK. Well they're there now.
And there's guns and all.
Two of the boys got word.
That's why they stopped me this morning.
We're under orders.
We're not to drive this train.

JANE. Not to drive this train?

JACK. Exactly

JANE. What do you mean 'exactly'?!

JACK. There's an embargo...

GRACIE. Fuck.

JANE. What embargo?

GRACIE. Would you bloody believe it.

JANE. Believe what?

JACK. We're not going anywhere, missus.

JANE. What do you mean?
What does he mean, mister?

GRACIE. We don't carry guns.
 And we don't carry soldiers.

JANE. Who doesn't?

GRACIE. We don't.
 Dockers and drivers.
 I don't.
 There's an embargo, a strike.
 It's country wide... it's been going on all summer.

JACK. We don't move their British killers round the country,
 missus.

JANE. No... Nooooo... this can't be... you can't be...

JACK. There's a whole bloody troop of them out there, Gracie.
 Bastards probably planned to board at the last minute.

GRACIE. Yeah... that's what they've been doing lately.

JACK. Trying to trick us...
 But the boys have them copped...

GRACIE. The boys...

JANE. What boys?

JACK. Irish Republican Army, missus...
 This'll be a right stand-off!

 He turns out of the scene.

 A right stand-off.
 One of many.
 Sure the whole country was in chaos.
 With strikes.
 Curfews.
 Shootings.
 Executions.
 Rampaging bastard Black and Tans.
 Ireland was **ablaze**.
 And with that fire came fury.
 Fury... fuelled by years of silent subjugation to **British
 thieves**.
 And I felt it.
 Felt it in me bones I did.

And I felt that we could – (JANE *says this word too*.) **win**.
I felt that this was our time.
So when I got that tip-off.
When I was told that our train was to be filled with soldiers,
British soldiers. I was only fucking thrilled.
I was only chomping at the bit.
To add to the mayhem.
To make my mark.

Switch back to the scene.

GRACIE. We'll have to find another way, missus.
    To get you out.
    This train can't go to Belfast.

JACK. There'll be no one going to Belfast.

JANE. No... no... please...

JACK. I knew Gracie was one of the drivers that supported the
    embargo.
    I knew Gracie was one of us.
    Despite the fact that he had fought in France.
    Despite the fact that he once wore the enemy uniform.
    I knew, we knew... word was... that he was true.
    Sure his brother was a top man in **Cork**.
    (GRACIE *says this too*.) **Jay Grace. A legend** if the truth be
    told.
    Wreaking havoc out there in the wilds of Skibbereen, Goleen
    and Bantry.

GRACIE. Burning bridges, burning barracks, my wee brother
    Jay was a master of the ambush. They say he ran the RIC out
    of Ballymurphy, out of Bandon, Ballincollig...

JACK. Ballywhere-ever-to-fuck, West Cork was now a no
    man's land for the Brits, all thanks to – (GRACIE *says this
    with* JACK.) **Jay Grace**. And so our boys could pick off
    soldiers and polis at random... from behind gorse, from
    behind rocks and from behind every little farm house in the
    county of Cork. They were a law unto them-fucking-
    selves... and not a train of guns or soldiers got anywhere
    near the south.
    Jay Grace vouched for Gracie, so there was no man in the
    IRA that would question that despite him being a bit of a

(GRACIE *says this with* JACK.) **quare hawk**, a bit of a
pansy... hanging around the music halls and that...

GRACIE *sings the first verse of 'I Didn't Raise My Boy to Be
a Soldier' by Alfred Bryan.*

Sure none of them were right in the head were they?
When they came back from from the war. From France or
Flanders or Egypt or wherever.
None of them were ever the same.
The shelled-out faces. Stutterin', splutterin' poor legless
bastards... sure they were all over Dublin, all over the
country... stranded now, lost forever in no man's land after
fighting on the wrong side, in the wrong army, at the wrong
war.
Some said they only got what they deserved.
Some said they were codded into going to war.
Some said they were traitors to Ireland.
But not Gracie.
Gracie was fighting for us now.
And – (GRACIE *says this too*.) **Gracie had form**.

GRACIE. Just two weeks previous.

JACK (GRACIE *says this with* JACK). **On the Westmoreland
Street to Clones** Gracie refused to drive.
On account of rifles being part of the cargo.
And when no other driver would take his place, they say an
officer stepped up onto the footplate, put a gun to Gracie's
head and said 'You will get the contents of this revolver if
you don't drive' but Gracie just kept his hands in his pockets
and started singing.

GRACIE *sings the chorus of 'I Didn't Raise My Boy to Be a
Soldier'.*

The auld officer was apoplectic.
Cocked his trigger and all.
But Gracie never missed a note.
I love that story.
Loved it.

'What song was it you were singing?' I asked Gracie after
but he wouldn't say.

GRACIE. 'Sure we might torment them into leaving –'

JACK. – was all –

GRACIE. '– that would save on all the killing.'

JACK. A – (GRACIE *says this too*.) **quare hawk** all right.
With his tales of Ancient Greece and his mother.
With his singing and his… ways.
Gracie would rarely talk politics.
Said he'd had enough of that shite in the war.
Said he'd no love – (GRACIE *says this with* JACK.) **for
Sinn Féin or their sacred Republic,
…only Ireland**.
I said they were one and the same.
Gracie said he – (GRACIE *says this too*) **wasn't so sure**.

So when I think of it.
Of that day.
And then what they did to Gracie because of it.
In Kells.
Well I think that it should never have happened.
I think that it was just one of those things, one of those
moments, when stars cross or stars crash or stars whatever-
to-fuck… and people break… and people…

(JANE *says his name too*.) **Gracie** is my first ghost.
My first regret.
And I don't regret much.
I don't regret most of my killing.
It had to be done.
I'd do it all again in the fight for freedom.
But Gracie…?
I had no row with him.
I had no row with you…

*Return to the scene and first few lines are repeated exactly as
before.*

GRACIE. We'll have to find another way, missus.
To get you out.
This train can't go to Belfast.

JACK. There'll be no one going to Belfast…

JANE. No… no… please…

GRACIE. Have they set up alternative transport, Jack?

JACK. Have they what?

GRACIE. Sinn Féin? They usually set up a link to a different
line so as not to piss off all the passengers.
This train is bloody packed.

JACK. How would I know?

GRACIE. Well what exactly did they say to you?

JACK. I told you.
Guns and soldiers.
We're not to drive the train.

GRACIE. So maybe we could smuggle her out?

JACK. What?

GRACIE. Was there any police about?

JACK. Is half the British Army not enough for you?

GRACIE. She's not running from the army, she's running from
the police.

JACK. For what? What's she running for...

GRACIE. If we can smuggle her out, maybe we can get her
onto whatever link they've sorted to connect to another line?

JACK. Smuggle her how?

GRACIE. I don't know.
There's not a lot of time.

JACK. Is she some sort of relation, Gracie?

GRACIE. No...

JACK. Your bit of skirt?

GRACIE. For God's sake...

JACK. Then who the fuck is she?
Why do we have to be smuggling her out?
Haven't we enough to contend with?
Tell her to go on about her business...

He turns to JANE.

You'll have to go on about your business, missus.
This train is going nowhere.

JANE. But you said…
You promised…

GRACIE. I know I did…

JACK. Well you'll have to forget his promise.
This is war.
This is an embargo.
And we don't break strikes.

You mightn't understand that.
This action is for all our freedom.

JANE. I mightn't understand?
I mightn't understand!
Who the hell do you think you are, young fella?
Just out of short trousers and the snot on ya!
I've been standing under red flags since before you could
walk! Got me badge and me papers and years… years of it.
But then the red flag got wrapped in the green didn't it and
my dreams of equality became your dreams of an Irish
Republic.
So where the hell is it, this bleedin' Republic?
Coz it's all I hear of these days. On the streets and down the
lanes with posters plastered and pamphlets flying and
newspapers… and shootings… and raids.
Doors kicked in for this Republic, young fella!
And kids screaming, and kids murdered and mothers broken
and husbands dead and carnage yet I'm still waiting, still!
After years, almost ten years, young fella, of struggle and
meetings, of bullets and beatings and I still have nothing.
And me kids have nothing.
And I have to listen to you two, arguing over me head, like
I'm nothing!
Thinking that it's in your power to decide my fate.
Well that's some fucking Republic that is.
A Republic that thinks nothing of me.
Yet a Republic that owes me.
A Republic that took my husband and my youth.
But I'll tell you one thing! I'll not feed it me children too.

I'm finished with it.
Because if I get arrested.
If I go to jail.
My kids will starve.
So if you two need to liberate something.
And if you two believe in freedom like you say you do.
Then liberate me.

A whistle blows.
There are the sounds of marching.

GRACIE. That's the bloody soldiers now.

JACK. It is.

JANE. Jesus…

GRACIE. They'll be boarding the boxes.
I don't know what we can do for you now, missus.

JACK. She can slip through them.
Or jump another train.

JANE. Did you hear a word I said?

JACK. They'll be up to the cab in minutes, we'll tell them to go
fuck themselves, Gracie.

JANE. I asked you did you hear me?

JACK. I did. Of course I did. Sure aren't we nose to nose in this
bloody cab. But it makes no differ. You're not my problem.
I'm here for the Irish Republican Army.

JANE. I know that army. And I know who runs it.

And it's not Mick Collins or Mulcahy, no matter what you
think, I'm telling you it's the likes of Kiernan, Kiernan,
mister!

And those self-same bosses that spat on us during the lock-
out and tried to ban our unions, then brought in scabs and set
the polis and British Army itself upon us… but they are
wrapped now in the thickest of green and call themselves
Séan or Mícheál and they have Sinn Féin in their pocket and
every other eejit like you with a gun in his hand. Because
they're like weather cocks them boys and they know what

way the wind is blowing, so they're saddling up, just like the
clergy, saddling up to ride roughshod over us, that's me and
you young fella, and just you watch, they'll take charge of
this new Republic... and they'll make sure that their trams
and their hotels and their banks are all safe from your
revolution.

JACK. Would you tell her to shut up, Gracie.
For fuck's sake.
You don't know what you're talking about, missus.

JANE. But I do... I do, and I don't want to take your dreams
from ya, young fella.
I don't mean to.
Because I know your fire.
I can feel the heat from here.
But I need this train to go to Belfast or I'm finished.

JACK. Tough.
It won't be leaving this morning.

And with that the old witch sprang up... with a fucking
hook!
A hook! The likes of which I'd never seen before! And she
was like a lion. Eyes blazing and the nest of hair cut loose
and streeling round her face... she near took me bleeding
head off! But then Gracie – (GRACIE *says this with* JACK.)
**got her in his grip and she couldn't manage the two of us
so the hook fell on to the tracks and she fell back into the
corner**.

GRACIE.... like a rag doll.

JACK. You mad bitch!

GRACIE. Settle down... settle down, for God's sake, Jack.

JACK. She could have killed me!
I'm bleeding.

GRACIE. It's only a scratch.
You'll be grand.

JACK. What the fuck did she do anyway?
What the fuck has you running, missus, is it murder?

GRACIE. Near enough.

JACK. It is murder!
Jesus Christ.

GRACIE. From the sounds of who she killed she was doing the
Republic a favour.

JACK. Then get her out.
Will you, Gracie.
For God's sake.
We have real business here.

GRACIE. Will you be all right, missus?
Can you stand up?
Can you slip off, do you think, before the final whistle?

I can't drive it... I can't drive this train now and break the
embargo... there must be another way for you to get out of
Dublin. You'll have to go now because there'll be hell to pay
with them soldiers when we don't move off at ten.

JANE. No... I'm not goin'... I have no one, nowhere...

JACK. Here, I'll throw her off...

GRACIE. Leave her be Jack, for God's sake
Come on, missus, please, them officers will be up to the cab
like divils when we don't take off. And if they find you here,
they'll hand you over to the polis... or worse.

JANE. But you said you'd get me up to Belfast.

JACK. For Jesus' sake...

More whistles.

GRACIE. What's that?

Sound of whistles, commotion, boots.

JACK. It's polis. There's a few of them coming on up the
platform.

JANE. They're here for me

JACK. They're looking for someone all right.
Moving between the passengers.

JANE. That's it, I'm finished.

GRACIE. No you're not. There's time to run...
Come on now. Don't give up.

JANE. But I've no more running in me.

Don't you understand.
You were my last hope.
They'll put me back in Mountjoy for killing Kiernan.
And I'll die there this time.
I'm tired, mister, too tired.

GRACIE. And I knew she meant it.
I knew...
Because I've seen that light go out before...when men
succumbed to the promise of rest... when the incessant noise
and squalor and slaughter of war just became too much. I'd
have chosen death myself if the singing hadn't kept me away
from the front.
I knew there was nothing left in her.
So what could I do?
Leave the poor woman to her fate?
Let the polis have her?
Let her children starve?
When there would be other trains, other battles and other
frays I could take up for the Irish Republic?

GRACIE. Jack.

JACK. What?

GRACIE. I'm stoking her up.

JACK. You're what?

GRACIE. I made this woman a promise.
I'm going to drive the train.

JACK. But you can't.

GRACIE. There's polis everywhere.
Army everywhere.
She's done for if we don't leave...

JACK. But she's no one, nothing!

GRACIE. She's a person, for God's sake.
And she could be your mother, my mother!

JACK. So fucking what, Gracie? This is war!
And you know how war works. You know what this is
all for!
Come on now, we have the bastards on the run, finally...
after eight hundred fucking years... sure half the railway
lines are closed, they can't get their killers out to shoot our
boys. This is working. We have victory in our sights. And
every moment counts, every refusal... sure it's all we have
isn't it, our refusal... It WAS all we had... our refusal to be
fucking whipped... all we have, Gracie... is ourselves.

GRACIE. I don't know...

JANE. It's not for me, mister.
It's for my children.
They've no one else.
They'll die if I don't get to Belfast.

JACK. Would you ever shut up.

JANE. And with that he came at me...
With a **knife**.
I caught the glint of it – (GRACIE *says this with her.*) **in the
light of the coals**.

GRACIE. What are you doing?

JACK. She's getting in our way!

JANE. But Gracie had the measure of him.
And Gracie had the strength to crush him.
So Gracie knocked the knife right out of his hand...
And struck him to the floor...
Jesus!
Sweet suffering Jesus!

GRACIE. There'll be no more killing.
I said 'No more'.

JACK. O ya said that did ya?
Who'd ya say it to?
To the IRA was it? Or to your brother?

Your own brother who's out there fighting night and day.
Your own brother who tosses his life into the face of an
imperial army a thousand times the size of his own. That
self-same army you're now willing to drive about the place,
an army that murders us with impunity...

GRACIE. Stop it...

JACK. Stop what?

GRACIE. I won't hear it.
I won't hear any more.

JACK. Don't drive, Gracie.
Don't.
Their bullets will be used to kill our brothers.

GRACIE. For fuck's sake...

JACK. You're one of us now.

GRACIE. Am I?

JACK. Yes and listen, I feel sorry for this woman too.
I feel sorry for every last one of us has to live under the
enemy's boot. Isn't that why I'm here? Isn't that why we're
doing this... refusing to drive this train... our freedom is in
that refusal...

JANE. Not for me.
Not for me it isn't...

GRACIE. War is a bestial thing, Jack.

JACK. I'm not saying it isn't.

GRACIE. It's a bestial thing and there's no glory in it.

JACK. I know...

GRACIE. It devours, just devours...

JACK. I said I know...

GRACIE. But do you?
I'm telling you, Jack.
I've seen this all before...
War will leave only the husk of a man, the shell of a soul.

JACK. It has to be done.

GRACIE. No...

JACK. No exceptions, no excuses...

GRACIE. But war has all but destroyed this woman...
    All but destroyed me.

JACK. I don't care.

    Beat.

GRACIE. No.
    You don't care.
    You can't care.
    And maybe you're right.
    Maybe your Republic will be worth it.
    I hope so.

    The whistle goes.

JACK. That's ten o'clock.

JANE. What are you going to do, mister?
    What are you going to do?

GRACIE. She's earned her freedom... Jack.
    She's flesh and blood and love and honour.
    She just wants to save her kids.
    I'm driving to Belfast.

JANE. O thank God.

JACK. Then you're a fucking traitor.

GRACIE. Step out of the cab now, Jack.
    Take your stand.
    Refuse to work.
    I'll take the shit for this.

JACK. Damn right you will...

JANE. God bless you, mister.

JACK. Cowardly bastard...

GRACIE. Step out...
    Step out I tell ya...

JANE. So Gracie flung the boy out of the cab.

JACK. On your head be it!
(JANE *says this with* JACK.) **That shawlie will be your ruin.**
You fucking (GRACIE *says this with* JACK.) **queer**.
You'll be sorry.
You'll be sorry when the IRA hear...

JANE. Then the flagman waved.

GRACIE. And the train finally spluttered into life.

JACK. Carting guns and murderous bastards up to Belfast.

JANE. It was slow at first... the shift of the train... I almost didn't dare dream it... but with the two of us shovelling, Dublin eventually disappeared and a new and screaming green embraced us.

GRACIE. It was like the years fell off her as we sped north. The familiar sea-scapes and field gates and wild roses along the track erasing time and lifting the dread from off her shoulders.

JANE. Every station brought back a pocket of strength.

GRACIE. And all those faces of the men I couldn't save, couldn't carry away from the front, seemed to crowd onto that engine with us.

A slow sound of troops singing 'It's a Long Way to Tipperary' might start here, then fade but really hit intensity at the end of the play.

JANE. And he kept me hid, that gracious man.
That curious man.
And he shared the bite that he had with him.
And he sang old tunes.
'Til we could see the hills and heave of Belfast.

GRACIE. Where she disappeared.
Just a slip of a thing,
Another hem,
Another shawl,
Another soul,
into the soup of that city.

But not before she planted a kiss.
A blissfully soft uncomplicated kiss onto the face of this –
(JACK *says this with* GRACIE.) **traitor**.

JACK. '...He's a fucking traitor' I told the boys.
When I got home.
When I had to explain our failure.
Our failure in a time of rage.

And – (*Echoed by Jane and Gracie*.) **rage** is a curious event,
isn't it?
An eruption so great that it might change the course of a life,
just as lava might change the shape of a mountain.
It was **rage** that filled us in those years as we as counted the
cost of British tyranny and British plunder. And **rage** that
finally fuelled our guns, and tore at our hearts and choked up
the skies as a people we struck, and as a people we rose... to
change the course of our history.

But there is always a man, or a woman,
That gets hit in the fray.
Caught in the tug.
All but destroyed in the crossfire.

GRACIE. I thought they'd only give him a beating. That was
the usual punishment for breaking the embargo but Deavy
had a savage reputation. And there was something about
Gracie made Deavy go all out. Maybe on account of him
being ex-army... or on account of his 'ways'... but the boys
in Kells wouldn't be done, I heard, with a simple beating.
For Gracie.
It was the tar and the feather.

I was glad I hadn't to wait too long for whatever reprisal was
coming. I had made my bed and I was up for the fallout so
long as the lady Jane and her kids made it from Dublin to
Belfast to Liverpool and on with their living. And sure
enough as I left the railway men's dormitory, in Kells for
work only two days later, what do I see but a group of 'the
boys' waiting outside. And I knew that they must have been
sent to deliver.
Flat caps and burning cheeks.
They reminded me of myself,

Or what I might have been if I hadn't ended up in France.
They reminded me of my brother.

I went with their little posse without objection.

JANE. And I often think of him now.
And his bird-like face.
And his gentle eyes.
I owe him my life
And the beautiful life of my children.

JACK. A beating.
All he deserved was a real good beating.

GRACIE. **But no.**
They chose to dress me in white…
Like a bride to two wars.
Two wars I had no stake in.
The Irish Republic had no more love for me than the ancient
foe. Deavy's venom and IRA boots were brutal enough to
prove that.
Prove that there'd be no place in Ireland for the likes of me.
Gracie Grace was fashioned in the mayhem of France.

The ghostly singing rise in tempo during GRACIE'*s last
speeches…*

(*Echoed by* JANE *and* JACK.) **Rage**
is a curious event, isn't it?
And it was – (*Echoed by* JANE *and* JACK.) **rage** that
spurred me on as I tore up every seat and every board in that
wretched railway station. **Rage** as I thought of the love of
my mother.
Rage as I thought of the senselessness of her poverty and her
life… and mine…

But then I heard them.
I heard my old pals, my old troupe from the trenches.
And suddenly I could see them.
The ghost of them.
Sitting aboard the engine of the oncoming train.
Singing in the wind, they were.

*The song gets higher and with it the sound of a train until it
hits a crescendo on his last line.*

Singing for me.
And all I had to do to join them was to soar.
All I had to do was to lift up my wings.
Like Icarus.
And fly into the face of it.
The face of that oncoming train.
Then I was free.

JACK. They say that he jumped.
Right into the path of a 'special'...
It wasn't stopping in Kells so... there wasn't a hope.
They say there was little or nothing left of him.

JANE. And so we return... to feel it all again.
Tell it all again.

JACK. Ghosts.

JANE. Spectres of the passions that once drove the world.

GRACIE. Flickers of history.

JACK. Phantoms of war.

JANE. **Because our struggles, our loves, our stories are
yours.
Before we melt away.**
Back into the walls of time.

End.

OUTRAGE

The Civil War (1922–23)

Dedicated to the memory
of my own
Róisín

Characters

ALICE
NELL
PJ

Note on Text

When lines are in bold there is an element of choral speaking.

Commisioned by Meath County Council Arts Office.

ALICE/NELL/PJ. The sundering came slow at first.

PJ. In grumbling on street corners.
Voices raised in the heat of a public house.

NELL. Darts of accusation in jaded rebel eyes.

ALICE. But then you could see it take hold.
Take hold like a creeping contagion,
snaking through the countryside.
The sundering was like a blight rolling in on the mist.
A scourge

PJ.…that whipped up anger, dissent and discord
amongst towns, families, columns, councils, courts,

ALICE.…lovers and friends.

PJ. Lines were being drawn now right through Irish households.
Irish villages.
Irish hearts.

NELL. It was civil war.
Civil war…

PJ. Despite our best efforts to avoid it.

NELL. **Pat Finney.**

PJ. **Pat Finney.**

ALICE. **Pat Finney.**

NELL. He came for me in the heat of it.
The fire of it.
The curse of it.

PJ. The curse of civil war.

NELL. The first night that I saw him was at the burning of
Castle Saunderson, when we were all still of the one army,
all still of the one mind. One of our blackened faces grinning
in the moonlight.

ALICE/PJ. **Finney.**

NELL. He came and knelt right beside me to peer through the
thorn, to thrill at the sight of the blaze taking hold. O and
how we thrilled at our bonfire of the vanities. Our bonfire of
arrogance, privilege, greed. How we thrilled to watch
another colonial mansion burn. To hear the old house scream
and crash and spit into the night sky. I remember I didn't
want to leave. I didn't want to turn my back on that
inferno... the glory of it, the justice.
Yes –

ALICE. He was with you then.

NELL. He was with us then.

PJ. **Finney.**

NELL. Growing in confidence,
in violence.
He slipped his arm about my shoulder but I didn't respond.
War makes heroes and demons, doesn't it?
So how could war in Ireland be any different?
No matter what the priests say.
Or the Staters.
Or the books.

PJ/ALICE. Heroes and demons.

NELL. I was organising in County Cavan for Cumann na mBan
when I got that chance to see Castle Saunderson burn. I was
active throughout the Tan War. Active, if the truth be told,
since first I got a job as a baker's assistant on Talbot Street in
1902, when I came across the resplendent Maud Gonne and
her women's political movement. I was little more than a
child at the time, thirteen, but joined up with Inghinidhe na
hÉireann and that set me on my course through this world.

ALICE. **Pat Finney.**

NELL. **Pat Finney.**

ALICE. I had met him once in Dublin, I'm sure of it.
When I was delivering a despatch to a group of ministers.
I can see still see him in my mind's eye, seated among them,

all elbows and knees, sprung! I didn't like the look of him, the way he ate me up entirely with his eyes but I could see that he was well thought of by the men, well respected...

NELL. As one of our most efficient killers.

ALICE. At the heart of our war with Britain.

NELL. **Finney.**

PJ. I never knew him before that night.
Never met him in all my skirmishes, battles, ambushes, through the years. Not even when he was training recruits down home in Meath –

ALICE. **Finney.**

PJ. – though I had heard whispers of his... *talents*. His name was well known in the IRA even if he never courted the limelight.
And his name was feared.

NELL. One of them that had grand plans for himself for when the fight was over.

ALICE. The fight.

It was my sister Nell that first brought Ireland's fight into our home. Wrapped up carefully in her baker's apron.
Hot on her floury hands.
And she found willing recruits in us siblings.
Much to our mother's bewilderment.
And much to our mother's cost.
My mother lost two of her sons to bullets on O'Connell Street.
Then there was Nell.
And then there was me.

PJ. Alice.

NELL. Alice.

ALICE. Drawn into the excitement of revolution like a moth to a flame.

PJ. Even though there were nearly ten years between them, Nell was more than a sister to Alice, she was her goddess, her compass. Not me. I think she would have followed Nell through to the gates of hell.

ALICE. I was writing for the *Irish Bulletin* in the department of Propaganda of Ireland's first Dáil when I met PJ.

PJ. The department being the illegal arm of our illegal government consisting of two typewriters and courageous youth.
For me it was love at first sight.
For Alice…

ALICE. It might have taken a little longer.

PJ. I had fierce competition you see from Nell and 'the fight'.

They switch now to a scene, the scenes and direct address spin effortlessly around each other.

NELL. Read me the latest so.

ALICE (*coughs and holds up her sheet*). 'It is stated by the English cabinet minister that the "stern measures" taken by the English Government in Ireland are directed at a "small body of assasins", "a numerically insignificant group of terrorists", "a handful of extremists". The fact is that the "stern measures" are taken against the whole people of Ireland, and their object is not the suppression of crime but the breaking of the spirit of the Irish nation.'

NELL. Good.
If a bit formal.

ALICE. Formal?

NELL. Stiff.

ALICE. I know what it bloody means… I just… we have to be 'formal' if we are to be respected as a real source of real news!

NELL. I prefer it when you write them like stories.

ALICE. Stories? Is it Hans Christian Andersen you're after?

NELL. You should write about that poor woman in Galway.

ALICE. I did write about that poor woman in Galway.

NELL. Mowed down by the Black and Tans as they drove by her door.

ALICE. I know.

NELL. Standing minding her own business she was… and her four children 'round her.

ALICE. I wrote about her in Tuesday's bulletin. Dublin Castle called her murder 'death by misadventure' but we got the truth out…

NELL. You need to get the bulletin out ahead of their lies.

ALICE. That's easier said than done Nell!

NELL. We have to be a step ahead… you know that…
Always a step ahead –

ALICE. Or we're dead.
I do. I know that.

PJ. Alice's department worked out of one of them big houses on Harcourt Street.

ALICE. Number six Harcourt Street.

PJ. And I was sent up to report an atrocity committed on a local girl by a British Sergeant.

ALICE. Because the bulletin specialised in publishing the true nature of British military activity around the country.

PJ. The Sergeant in question had apparently compromised the girl before placing a gun in her mouth in a bid to make her disclose the whereabouts of her IRA brother.

NELL. The bastard!

PJ. The girl was distraught and too ashamed to recount the event herself so the CO sent me up to Dublin to tell the tale.

NELL. Attacks like that were happening throughout the country.

ALICE. And we needed the world to know about it.

NELL. When he finished the testimony PJ should have left the building…

PJ. ...but I didn't. I sat down in the hall of number six waiting for Alice Farrell to finish her shift, to invite her to Mitchell's of Grafton Street for a cup of tea and cake.

ALICE. I ate all round me.

PJ. She did! She ate all round her – (*He laughs*.) cleaning me out of my few coppers so that I had to walk all the way back to my digs by the south docks, but I didn't mind, I would have walked to Jupiter and back just to spend another hour with her, the sheer delight of Alice Farrell.

ALICE. PJ then began to show up at the office of the *Irish Bulletin* more often than the bloody Black and Tans so I thought I better walk out with him... even if it was only for the feed!

PJ (*laughs again*). I'd like to think the attraction was a bit stronger than that.

ALICE. Though the attraction might have been just a bit stronger than that!

NELL. Myself and Alice were in the thick of the Republican movement in Dublin so PJ moved up from Meath to train in making explosives.

PJ. I was love-struck.

ALICE. Love-struck!

NELL. He had been running with a small column at home in Meath.

PJ. I had, I'd been running with a small column at home. We were keen but we saw little action because we had feck-all guns.

NELL. That was the curse of the Irish freedom fighter in those years, not a gun between them.

PJ. I had attached myself to the Kells Battalion from school and spent most of 1919 breaking and entering farmyards, big houses, barns and kitchens with my best pal Jimmy Swan from Clongill trying to find firearms. There was many a mad dash through the fields I can tell you with buckshot or bullets whizzing after us.

NELL. So they took to making bombs.

PJ. We did. We took to making bombs. Out of old cannisters or scrap metal, powder and fuse.

ALICE. And he was a dab-hand at it.

PJ. I suppose!

NELL. Talented.

PJ. But Meath was a relatively quiet county apart from the antics of the crowd up above in Dunboyne. I grew frustrated by our inaction. Frustrated by the caution, fear, inertia I could sense in my gentle neighbours and the absolute refusal of my own father to have any truck with 'them blasted rebels' or Sinn Féin. My da worked as a gardener for the Headford Estate, he loved the place and we lived in a small cottage by the good grace of Lord Headford himself so my da was hardly likely to go to war now with them that gave him a living… still I was me own man and I believed strongly in the fight for freedom. I had attended speeches in the town square over the years with Jimmy by such luminaries as Roger Casement, Francis Sheehy Skeffington and the Countess Markevitz herself. I had read every publication and pamphlet I could lay hand on and loved to sing all the old ballads during Gaelic League nights with the madman Brian O'Higgins from out by Kilskyre. I was filled full with it all… the excitement, the hope, the grievance so I thought to throw my lot in with the crowd down at Dublin Port where a cousin of me mother's was a commandant.

NELL. Third Battalion, Dublin Brigade.

PJ. That's it.

NELL. Commended for their efforts in smuggling, murder and espionage.

PJ. We were stationed in a small pump house at the heart of the port, a seasoned enough crew of spies and gunmen. All Dubs mostly and all true. I was happy there. Much happier to take up the fight in Dublin because in Dublin we weren't just tormenting the local polis, I had little heart for that…

NELL. The local polis were spies for the British.

PJ. Not all of them.

ALICE. Enough of them.

PJ. Well to me they felt like neighbours. At least in Dublin we got to go head to head with the big boys, the real Brits... Imperial forces...

NELL. Black and Tans.

PJ. Auxies.

ALICE. And Dublin Castle.

PJ. Yes, Dublin Castle.

NELL. Dublin Castle was the head of British administration in Dublin with her own ministry for propaganda.

ALICE. So we took them on.

NELL. We took them on.

PJ. Two typewriters and courageous youth.

ALICE. The duties of my position included writing for the bulletin, making copies, distribution and at times taking notes or dictation from Irish Government ministers or even from Mr Arthur Griffith himself, Ireland's President.

PJ. Alice worked from morning until night.
She loved it.

ALICE. I loved it.

NELL. And printing her tales of British military depravity began to prove a right scourge to the Castle so they came after her and her colleagues regularly and with gusto!

ALICE. We had to shift premises that many times that my typewriter almost developed feet of its own! It was like we were always packing... packing papers, packing pamphlets, transcripts, briefcases and monies at a moment's notice to run, sometimes under gunfire to another location. The bulletin had thirteen premises in all during the war. Thirteen!

NELL. Unlucky for some.

PJ. And I followed her as a bomb-maker and a soldier and a
lover to every one.
They were dangerous days.

NELL. Feverish days.

ALICE. But thrilling all the same because we believed, we
really believed that a new Irish Republic held a future for us
all.

NELL. Men, women and children.

PJ. Just like Padraig Pearse had declared to an empty street
back in 1916.

Beat.

ALICE. But **Finney**

NELL. **Finney**

PJ. **Finney...**

ALICE. I tried to keep my hands down.
I tried to keep my arms around my belly.
I begged... I...

PJ. Stop.
Please stop!

NELL. Alice...

PJ. Alice...

Slight pause.

Alice Farrell was like a magnet.
Surrounded. Admired. And the size of her! Like a hurricane
in miniature, pounding at the typewriter, flushed, fast, or
whirling through the streets of Dublin on her bicycle, a
despatch nesting in her hair or a mountain of pamphlets in
her satchel... you could barely see her sometimes for
fervour... was like a shock... an explosion all of her own...

ALICE. PJ was strong and steady.
PJ was always there... always ready to put the hand out and
hold me. Fine, strong hands.

PJ. What kind of time is this to be finishing work?
I'm afraid that auld Irish Republic might be taking
advantage.

ALICE (*laughs*). Have you been waiting outside all night?

PJ. Sure weren't we supposed to be going to the pictures?

ALICE. Were we?
I'm sorry. I forgot entirely.
We had to finish today's edition...

PJ. Well you might win the war for us yet.
Your little rag is causing as much chaos for the British as
Mick Collins!

ALICE. The *Irish Bulletin* is no rag.

PJ. Not at all, sure it's pure poetry with all them tales of
beating, burning, drinking, shooting...

ALICE. And isn't it about time that the world knew what the
British are at in Ireland?!

PJ. Absolutely it is but isn't it also time for us to be having a
little drink, or a bite?

ALICE. O, PJ, you should have told me you were coming, I've
to be up early!

PJ. I did tell you!

ALICE. I don't remember...

PJ. Will I just have to come back to your little flat so? You
know how I love all them books you have stacked in the
corner.

ALICE. O yes that's right, you like to come back to my little
flat for the books.

PJ. I'll be quiet as a mouse.

ALICE. YOU!

PJ. Sure what can I do with you so gorgeous and...

ALICE. Stop... would ya stop it...
Will you cycle so?... I'm shattered.

PJ. I will of course.
Hop up on that saddle and I'll have us home in a jiff.

ALICE. Well you better be quiet, if Mrs Kelly gets a whiff of you again I'll be evicted.

PJ. She won't I promise.
Come on.

ALICE. Come on yourself, I'm frozen.

PJ. Arms tight around me so...

She laughs.

NELL. They were married by the end of the summer.

PJ. 1921.

ALICE. After the truce was signed.

NELL. The truce between our provisional Irish Government and the British.

PJ. We were married and moved back home to Kells.

ALICE. With a little baby stirring...

PJ. A baby?!

ALICE. Isn't that what I just said.

PJ. A baby?!

ALICE. I think so...

PJ. Christ.

ALICE. Christ is right, I thought you were careful.
And I was SO careful!
How on earth did this happen, PJ?!

PJ. Well I think I might have an idea.

ALICE. Don't laugh at me!
I'm four weeks late.
What are we going to do?

PJ. Get married of course.

ALICE. Married?

PJ. Yes

ALICE. But... but I don't want to get married.

PJ. What?

ALICE. I'm too busy.
How will they survive at the office?

PJ. The office?

ALICE. It's too tricky a time...
What with the truce and all...

PJ. The truce... is that really what you're thinking of?... Now?

ALICE. What if it fails?
What if we go back to war?
How can I be having a baby, PJ?

PJ. The truce won't fail, Alice.
Sure we're all delighted with it.
The war is over, it's over and you've done your bit, more
than your bit, we can go home.

ALICE. Home?

PJ. To Kells.

ALICE. Kells?! What are you talking about?

PJ. Marry me, Alice. One of the uncles has a little printing shop
on Reilly Street and he wants me in to run it. The arthritis
has him killed and he says that I can take over the business
entirely if I can make a fist of it. We could set up house...

ALICE. What?

PJ. In Kells!

ALICE. But this is my home, Dublin is my home!
Jesus, how long have you been plotting this?

PJ. Plotting what?
Isn't it you that just up and told me that you think you're
pregnant!
And sure you know the mother has been after me for months
to get me home. She's my mother, Alice, and they're my

family and they miss me, despite it all and I'll tell you I miss
them, I miss home, Alice. And sure what am I doing... what
are we doing here if it's all over?

ALICE. Over? What's over? There's nothing over! Hostilities
could erupt again at any moment, I mean the Tans aren't off
the streets yet are they? No, no. I'm not ready, I'm not ready
for this at all, PJ!

PJ. But I don't see that you've got too much choice, Alice,
not if there's a baby there...

She gasps.

And if there's a baby there, I love it. I love it like I love you.
I can't live... I can't eat, Alice, I tell you I can barely breathe
unless I know I'm going to lie with you at night, every night,
you know that! Sure didn't I walk all the way home from
manoeuvres in Wicklow yesterday just to grab the last ten
minutes of darkness with you... don't tell me that you don't
love me? Please don't tell me that!

ALICE. Of course I love you.
Of course I do.

PJ. Thank God. So go to a doctor to be certain and then we can
make a plan.

ALICE. Make a plan?
Jesus help us, why are you always so calm?
So bloody calm and so bloody good!

PJ. Not that good considering your condition...!

ALICE. This is a disaster.

PJ. No it isn't.
It's a baby.
Just a baby.

ALICE. But what will Mr Griffith say?

PJ. Mr Griffith?
(*He laughs.*) I'd have thought you'd be more worried about
your mother?

ALICE. My poor mother gave up on me years ago.

PJ. Well I reckon Mr Griffith will have more on his mind than our baby… what with the truce, the army and the negotiations with British.

ALICE. Exactly.
Who could trust Lloyd George?
It won't last.
The truce won't last.

PJ. It will, the army's exhausted, the country's exhausted!

ALICE. How can you say that?

PJ. Because they've had enough of the destruction, Alice, and enough of death. There won't be a house or a man or a village left standing if we don't call off this bloody war and the truth is that we're almost out of bullets.

ALICE. Don't say that.

PJ. I won't. I don't. I don't say it to anyone but it's the truth and I think this truce is good. I think they'll go, the British. I think they'll give us Ireland… we're too much trouble for them.

ALICE. Do you really think that?

PJ. I do, I do!… Freedom is coming, Alice.

ALICE. I don't even dare dream it.

PJ. Just marry me will you?
Marry me and baby or no, we will be happy.

ALICE. I don't know…

PJ. You can still write your bulletin if there's a need for it.

ALICE. I can't give up.

PJ. We won't give up.
Not a chance.
We can have it all, Alice…

NELL. **But Finney…**

ALICE. **Finney.**

PJ. No.

ALICE. I tried to keep my hands down.
I tried to keep my arms around my belly.
I begged… I…

PJ. God… please no…

NELL. There were a right few IRA weddings the summer of the truce.
All bedecked with green ribbons and Celtic spirals and sashes and all the rest of that clobber. I can tell you I had grown to distrust all that Gaelic enthusiasm because it began to feel… religious… and needless to say I never trusted that either. Sure hadn't Irish priests and Irish bishops grown hoarse in their pulpits over the years forbidding any thought of revolution. The poor were just fodder for their God and the poor's pennies kept them in velvet and gold and starched cotton. No. No thank you, I was and always will be a Labour girl because 'The cause of Labour is the cause of Ireland and the cause of Ireland is the cause of Labour.' James Connolly knew that and James Connolly could see right through the priests and the Gaelic Leaguers especially them that 'used the green sunburst of Éirinn to cloak their rack-renting in the slums of Irish towns'. And I could see easy that the good Catholic merchants and Catholic landlords and Catholic bosses were getting all cosy with Griffith and his First Dáil, illegal or no, and I knew that if we weren't careful, they'd be bloody sitting in the Second Dáil, lording it over us, taking full control of our new Irish Republic, no better than the British.

PJ. The truce was a god-send.

ALICE. The truce was a strange time.

NELL. The truce was a curse.

ALICE. It kind of felt as if the world had stopped spinning after the truce, the world hit a bump in the road. And though most of the population were out celebrating, lighting bonfires, singing, I couldn't enter into their joy or pandemonium.
It was just the strangest feeling, like I was outside of myself. Locked outside of myself… in this strange little town of good neighbours and farmers and market-days and talk of cows, of fields and the price of grain.

I felt... stranded... because my world, my world of 'the fight' had so unexpectedly and immediately vanished, unexpectedly and immediately stopped. I remember waking in the middle of the night with PJ snoring happily beside me and I'd be formulating stories, reporting atrocities in my dreams, my fingers tap tap tapping on the ghost of a typewriter that sat silent now in an abandoned office in Dublin.

PJ. That summer of the truce was the happiest of my life. To have Alice home in Kells and all to myself. To watch her grow round like a little apple. To watch her plant lettuce and scallions and beetroot in the small garden between the house and the printing sheds, throwing out crumbs for the thrush and the wren and the blackbird. God I loved her. Love her still.

ALICE. PJ worked night and day to get that printing business back on its feet and I was supposed to make do with keeping house and preparing for the baby but in truth I didn't know what to be doing with myself. I still had one foot in my old life. I couldn't settle. It was like my world was in some class of hiatus and everything we had dreamed of, worked for, killed for hung in the balance.

PJ. I thought the war was over. Was glad the war was over because I just want, wanted our future, nothing special, just the joy that can be gleaned from a loving home and the freedom to prosper, to share love and happiness with your children.
But it wasn't to be.

ALICE. It wasn't to be.

NELL. Our army grew lazy with the truce.
Our army grew fat and boisterous with half of the young lads returning home to drink and boast and charm with tales of their military antics. Could they not see that if it all kicked off again we'd need them in ship-shape?
I was disgusted by it.
Disgusted by them.
Though not all of them slacked I'll admit that and the women of Cumann na mBan certainly didn't stand down.

Not a chance! Sure what had changed for us? We were still
expected to dance to the men's orders. We were still running
soup kitchens, caring for prisoners, gathering guns. There
was a road to go. I could see that. All of the Cumann na
mBan could see that, sure we were at nothing 'til we saw
what Collins brought home from those endless negotiations.

She is interrupted by the old-fashioned ring of a telephone.

ALICE. Nell. Is that you?

NELL. Of course it's me.
Didn't you just ask Mrs Woods to get me?

ALICE. Yes. Yes. I did.
So how are you?

NELL. How am I?
I'm grand, Alice...

ALICE. And how's Mrs Woods?

NELL. She's grand too. What is it? Is there something wrong?

ALICE. No, no.

NELL. So why did you telephone?
You know I don't trust this bloody thing...

ALICE. Because I was wondering... and PJ was wondering...
would you not think of coming down to us for a visit?

NELL. What?

ALICE. To Kells.

NELL. Jesus, Alice... what on earth would I be doing in Kells?

ALICE. It's a grand little town.

NELL. Well I'll take your word for it but sure I've no business
in it!

ALICE. Haven't you a sister in it!

NELL. What's wrong with you... are you all right?

ALICE. Yes!

NELL. And is PJ all right?

ALICE. He's grand, he's grand...

NELL. The baby?

ALICE. He's coming soon...

NELL. I know that... isn't it Christmas, you said?

ALICE. Yes. Christmas. It's just I want to see you... I want... ah go on, come down to us, Nell, there's lovely walks by the river here and there's dances!

NELL. Dances? Sure I've no interest in dances!

ALICE. Well we could play cards then or there's a picture house in Navan.

NELL. What are you talking about?

ALICE. Or PJ's brother has a horse! You've always wanted a go on a horse.

NELL (*to the audience*). I did actually! I always wanted a go on a horse!

ALICE. Come down will you, Nell, please? I'm getting as big as a house and the people here are lovely but it's not the same what with PJ working all hours and... and I'm just dying to hear all the news from Dublin. Will you not come down and just see me through the birth. Please. I miss you. I miss everything, Nell.

NELL. What could I do? My mother couldn't go down because she still had nippers of her own and me da to contend with so I put my bicycle on the train and headed down to Alice's grand little town.

PJ. You're welcome, Nell.

NELL. And you're getting fat, Mr PJ Reilly.

PJ (*laughing*). Sweet as ever I see.

NELL. You're glad to be home then?

PJ. I am.

NELL. Where's Alice?

PJ. I didn't want her to be dragging herself out in the rain.
She's got a right bump on her now.

NELL. Has she? I still can't imagine Alice.

PJ. She's in good form though.
So delighted with your coming down.

NELL. I'll be happy to see her myself.
I brought her a coffee slice out of Bewley's.

PJ. Her favourite.

NELL. I know.
So how's the training going?

PJ. What training?

NELL. Training, PJ. I presume you're out with the young
bucks...

PJ. No.

NELL. What do you mean 'no'?

PJ. There's not too much call for action round here, Nell, never
was and sure isn't it over now, they're negotiating the finish
in London, we're all enjoying the bit of quiet.

NELL. 'Quiet'?
So are you telling me you're not out training?

PJ. Not regular.

NELL. Jesus!

PJ. What is this? An inquisition?
Amn't I trying to get a business going.

NELL. A business? What's got into you, PJ?
Don't you know that it's touch and go with the negotiations.
This truce could fail and then we'll all be back in combat in
weeks.

PJ. I hope not.

NELL. For God's sake!
Who's the CO in the town?

PJ. Would you not be more concerned about your sister?

NELL. Alice is grand… isn't she?
She said she was grand when she telephoned Mrs Woods.

PJ. She's looking forward to seeing you, Nell.
She's been baking since morning.

NELL. Baking? Alice?

PJ. Look! Can we not just play at being civilians?

NELL. Why would we want to do that?

PJ. At least until the baby comes?
Will you stay until the baby comes?

NELL. I said I would, didn't I!

ALICE. But the baby –

PJ. James –

ALICE. – had barely turned his sweet face to the world when
the Treaty between Lloyd George and Ireland was
announced.

NELL. Then all hell broke loose.

PJ. All hell.

ALICE. All hell.

I don't know what to think?
I mean what exactly is a '*Free State*'.

NELL. Well whatever it is, it isn't a Republic.

PJ. They're calling it a *stepping stone*.

NELL. Is that what my brothers died for?
A stepping stone?
Some class of a half-promise?

PJ. Ah, Nell, we need to give it a chance!

NELL. Give what a chance exactly?
I can see little or no detail –

PJ. Sure the ink is barely dry on it.

NELL. Well, Collins and the boys better stay where they are 'til they get Lloyd George to sign up to what we've all been fighting and dying for, an Irish Republic!

ALICE. It says here in the paper that that there's no hope of getting back the North? We're to give it up entirely.

NELL. I know! Partition!
For God's sake, partition, PJ?!

PJ. I know. I know.
There's no need to be shouting.

NELL. Who's shouting?

ALICE. How on earth did they agree to partition?

PJ. Maybe it won't last.
I mean, how can it? A handful of counties...

NELL. A handful of counties where the nationalists will be run out.

ALICE. Aren't they already run out... burnt out of their homes in Londonderry.

NELL. It's a total betrayal.

PJ. Is it?

ALICE. I don't know... they must have had no choice, no choice at all if even *Collins* signed it.

PJ. It's a start... that's all it is... and sure isn't it better than nothing, I mean it's better than Home Rule?!

NELL. Jesus... that says it all...

PJ. I don't know, Nell... I don't want to jump to any conclusions... we'll just have to see what's what...

NELL. It's a bloody disaster that's what's what...

ALICE (*reading*). 'Catholic families fleeing over the border'...!

PJ. Awful.
Awful.

ALICE. I don't know what to think...

PJ. There's holes in it for sure.
I'd imagine some of the men will be tearing mad over it.

NELL. I'm tearing mad over it!
It's capitulation!

ALICE. Do you really think so?

NELL. I do, and the army won't have it.
The army can't have it...

ALICE. But isn't it signed already?...

PJ. In lieu of a vote... there has to be a vote here doesn't there?

NELL. You're right.
There has to be a vote.
We still have a chance...

ALICE. To what? To stop it?

NELL. Yes, we still have a chance to stop it.
We just have to get organised.

PJ. And so Nell was away up to Dublin...

ALICE. And I didn't blame her. I'd have been the same myself
if it wasn't for James.

PJ. James Reilly.

ALICE. Six and half pounds of joy and dimples and smiles. O,
dear God, he was like a sunburst, a shaft of light in the dead
of that winter and I adored him... despite it all, despite the
disappointment of the treaty and the rising rancour
throughout the country, I woke up to him each and every
morning. And that made me believe, for the briefest of
interludes, that peace might yet be at hand, that the 'stepping
stone' of a treaty might just succeed.

PJ. Meetings were held in every town and every village in
Ireland and it seemed to me that we were nearly all in
support of it. Certainly in Meath. We knew that it wasn't
perfect but we could see it as a means to an end and the men
in action wanted to get home to their farms, to their
sweethearts and their new families, they wanted to leave the
arguing to the politicians.

ALICE. It had been a brutal few years and you could see the debris of it, the hurt of it, in every man and woman's eyes.

PJ. I'm not saying Meath had suffered anything like the atrocities of Dublin or the west but some of our men had been on the run for years. They had lost jobs, brothers, sisters, homes. Some had done long stints in prison and once marked out as IRA had had to endure the terror meted out on their families by Auxies and Tans. It was almost four years of burning, murder and terror...

ALICE. Men shot. Women humiliated.

PJ. It had to be stopped.

NELL. But not like this.
And not with this Treaty.

PJ. I wanted to believe in it.

ALICE. I wanted to believe in it.

NELL. While there were some of us just didn't believe in it at all.

ALICE. And so the sundering came,
Slow at first,
In grumbling on street corners.

PJ. Voices raised in the heat of a public house.

NELL. Darts of accusation in jaded rebel eyes.

ALICE. And so **Finney**.

PJ. **Finney.**

NELL. **Finney.**

ALICE. Found his moment.
Made his mark.

NELL. Like all of us, Patrick Finney picked his side.
Patrick Finney weighed it all up and threw in his lot in with the Staters, them that accepted the treaty, accepted the Irish Free State.

ALICE. And so my fate was sealed.

The country felt all uneasy for months.
Fractious.

PJ. With meeting after meeting in Dublin, Tipp, Cork, Belfast
and everywhere else... trying to find common ground...
trying to keep the movement together but the break-up
couldn't be stopped...

ALICE. No, it couldn't be stopped.
The ghost of the dead seemed to sit on every man and
woman's shoulder. Some pleading for peace, others pleading
that their sacrifice not be forgot.

NELL. I found it excruciating.

ALICE. Excruciating.

NELL. Our future, our fight, slowly disintegrating as our army
and our leaders tore each other apart. Lloyd George must
have laughed his way back to Downing Street for he had
divided us entirely with that bloody Treaty.
I couldn't stick it.

ALICE. I couldn't stick it.

Nell and her comrades from Cumann na mBan took it in
shifts to lobby those that had a vote in the new Dáil to vote
down the Treaty and not give up on our Republic. I took the
train up and joined them once or twice in their hollering and
marching, little James in my arms... PJ came too but just to
hear the speeches... to hear it all argued out.

PJ. The Dáil voted to accept the Treaty –

NELL. Only by seven... seven bloody votes!

PJ. – they put it to the people in the summer of '22.

ALICE. And the people voted for it too.

PJ. That was enough for me.

ALICE. But not for Nell and not for a sizeable few.

NELL. I can't believe it... can't believe the people went and
swallowed that Treaty...

ALICE. They're just exhausted, Nell.
They want to build back their homes and villages.
They want peace.

PJ. We all want peace, that's what we all want...

ALICE. But it's no good if we aren't all in it together.

NELL. There's enough of us says no.

ALICE. But it will be civil war then... civil war!

PJ. It can't be.

NELL. Might have to be.

PJ. What are you saying, Nell?

NELL. You were there... you were there ragin' in the fire same as
me, PJ, and how many, how many friends and fellas and
innocents did we see die?... We can't do this, we can't have
this, this treaty betrays every one of them and every one of us!

PJ. So what do you suggest? That we all go out to kill again? And
kill each other this time? Are you mad? Are you gone mad-
cracked altogether to think that I could lift a gun against
another Irish man? Against a man that once fought by my side?

NELL. Well you might find he's not slow in lifting a gun
against you if you refuse to jump into line.

PJ. They've debated it.
They've voted it.
The Treaty's the best we could get.

NELL. It's not enough.

PJ. It is, Nell.
It has to be.

ALICE. Jimmy Swan won't support it.

PJ. What?

ALICE. Jimmy Swan was in the shop yesterday collecting
posters for the Race Meeting and he says the Treaty's a
sell-out.

NELL. He's right.

ALICE. He says he's seen too many die to give up now.
And he says he won't take any oath to the King of England.

PJ. Jimmy Swan doesn't have a family, Alice.

NELL. And doesn't having a family make it all the more
important?
Unless you want your children to be chattel just like
yourself?

ALICE. On and on and on it went.
The arguing.
The disagreement.
My heart was torn asunder.
Families were torn asunder.
All was war again.

PJ. All was war again.

NELL. 'Stepping stone' I'll give them their 'stepping stone' and
I'll fire it right back in through the windows of Westminster!

ALICE. So Nell went back to her room at Mrs Woods' house on
Moorehampton Road

NELL. Arming, recruiting, organising.
Just as before.

ALICE. But nothing.
Nothing could ever be... just as before.

NELL. It was in Mrs Woods' that I came head to head again
with **Finney**.

PJ. **Finney.**

ALICE. **Finney.**

NELL. He knew Mrs Woods' house well. Hadn't he slept in the
front room many the night after a raid or an ambush or some
such action during the Tan War. And he knew that Mrs
Woods and I, always successful in procuring weapons from
rogue British soldiers on the Curragh, were back up to our
tricks.

PJ. But now Nell was arming the forces against the Treaty.
The forces against the Free State.

ALICE. Against him.

NELL. Finney knew we always left a window open front and
back at Mrs Woods', so that anyone in action during the war
could slip into the house for a bit of heat or to find a corner
to sleep. And there was always bread and ham and tea at the
ready for our rebel guests who could stock up on weapons
too before they left. Indeed it was Mrs Woods gave me my
own little Wesson which I keep in the pocket of my skirt to
this day.

PJ. Yes Finney and the new Free State Army knew all the safe-
houses, all the trap-doors, false ceilings, open windows
because they had scrambled through them so many times
themselves. They were on to Mrs Woods...

ALICE. And on to Nell.

NELL. The bastards came crashing in one night... all bluster
and swagger and curses in their shiny new boots and buttons
and Free State guns. I told them to fuck off out of the place
but Mrs Woods, ever the lady, greeted Finney like a long-lost
friend...
(*As Mrs Woods*.) 'Patrick! Is that you in a splendid new hat?!
It is! Well now, how dashing. It's been too long, honestly,
and who could have foreseen such a state of affairs with you
and I and the army all split like this. It's dreadful. Dreadful it
is! And tell me how is Máire, I believe she had twins, what
joy... that's quite a brood you have now... you must be
exhausted between it all and the war and the endless
argument, why don't you sit yourself down and join myself
and Nell for a sup of tea, and your boys of course... are we
acquainted?... They look so terribly young... would they
like cake?'

She laughs.

At first Finney didn't know what to do with such a reception
but then he copped that Mrs Woods was probably only
delaying so sent some of his dogs on up the stairs and into
the front room to arrest any Anti-Treaty fighter might be

hiding out with us. There was pandemonium and shots fired, so I thought to take the opportunity to jump out the open window but Finney caught me by the waist –

PJ *(as* FINNEY). 'Nell, lovely Nell. What on earth am I going to do with you? Always raging about the place but I can't have ya jumping out that window can I? Sure you might hurt yourself –'

NELL. – and he manhandled me back inside, a sly grin plastered on his face. 'Traitor,' I spat back at him and kicked him hard in the groin.

PJ. Nell was dragged out into the street, thrown onto a truck and given ten months in Mountjoy.

NELL. Courtesy of the new Irish Free State.

ALICE. Hate reigned now.
Hate replaced brotherhood and sisterhood.
Hate seeped in through the walls, the thatch, the slate of every Irish home. Hate nestled in the coats and britches of every anti-treaty fighter. And hate marched in the green serge of the new Free State Army. I could no longer love this Ireland.

PJ. I could no longer love this Ireland.

ALICE. I no longer wanted it.

PJ. I hoped it might all peter out, the in-fighting but the truth is that there were some had a bit of a taste for it. Some, who almost enjoyed the carnage. Some, like **Finney.**

NELL. **Finney.**

ALICE. **Finney.**

NELL. He rose up through the ranks.

ALICE/PJ. **Finney**

NELL. Bloody Major General they made him while I lay stuck in Mountjoy.

ALICE. Mountjoy nearly killed her.

NELL. Executions.
Executions.
Executions.

PJ. There were so many... way too many...

ALICE. Executions.

NELL. The new Free State Army arresting, incarcerating and killing her own.

ALICE. O'Connor, Mellows, McKelvey, Dick Barrett.

PJ. All shot dead on the one morning in Mountjoy.

NELL. And I knew each and every one of those men well.

PJ. We all did.

ALICE. We had laughed with them, ran with them, cooked and drank and danced with them.

NELL. I heard the shot.
Every shot.

ALICE. Her nerves were never the same after...

NELL. My prison-mate Sheila and I scrambled up as best we could to the cell window every morning of the executions to scream and rage at the cowardly Free State bastards coming back, only to be treated to a folly of bullets aimed directly into our cell! We fell back down to our knees and Sheila began to say the rosary but I could never share her devotion or find comfort in them empty holy words.

PJ. The war raged.

ALICE. The war raged.

NELL. The war raged.

PJ. I didn't support the Anti-Treaty side, because I didn't believe that they gave the Treaty a chance but after the executions I couldn't support the Free State either. To stand a man against a wall. A man who devoted his life to the same ideal, the same Republic you did, and then to pin a marker on his heart only to blow it asunder... I couldn't... I just couldn't fathom...

ALICE. Then I got a letter from Mrs Woods.

I got a letter from Mrs Woods, PJ.
I've to go up to Nell.
She's gone on hunger strike.

PJ. Hunger strike?
Jesus, Alice, she'll die, sure there's little or nothing left of
her as it is.

ALICE. She wants to be treated as a prisoner of war.

PJ. Will you, for God's sake, talk to her?!
She just has to desist in this...

ALICE. What?
What, PJ? Is she not a prisoner of war?

PJ. She's... she's... don't know... I don't want it... I don't want
this...

ALICE. None of us want this but this is where your Treaty's
gone and brought us!

PJ. My Treaty? What's this? Since when did it become my
Treaty?
I'm as disappointed in it as you are, you know that... but the
country voted for it.

ALICE. Don't I know the country voted for it.
Don't I know! But I no longer care about the country, I only
care about my sister. So are you going to help me help my
sister, PJ?

PJ. Of course I am.

ALICE. Good.

PJ. I just, I just can't listen to it any more... read it any more...
it's like there is no end to the savagery... on both sides. A
seven-year-old boy burnt in his home in Stradbally only
yesterday, Jesus Christ! Just because his father took a seat in
the Senate...

ALICE. The IRA didn't know that he was in the house.

PJ. Imagine it was James...

ALICE. Don't...

PJ. A seven-year-old boy, Alice... what have we come to?

ALICE. I don't like it any more than you, PJ.
I want it to stop...

PJ. And they've killed Collins... Mick Collins?!
Sure, there'll be no one left, no one left at this rate!

ALICE. I know.
I hate it.
I hate it all too.

PJ. So come here and let me hold you.
I'll go with you. I'll go with you to Mountjoy.
We'll have to see if we can talk her out of it.

ALICE. Nell!?

PJ. But are you not afraid she'll die?

ALICE. Nell won't die. She can't.

NELL. The new Free State Guards in Mountjoy had learned
well from their old masters. They refused to confer on us the
status of soldier and refused to honour us as prisoners of war.
Jesus but they had some appetite for arresting! I'm telling
you there were more Irish citizens squashed into the cells of
Mountjoy in that year than there were abroad in the fields or
walking through the streets of their squalid little Free State.

ALICE. It seemed like half the country were behind bars.
Overcrowding was fierce and I was always afraid that Nell
might pick up TB or dysentry or worse.

NELL. The final straw for me was the day we refused to take a
fifth prisoner into our cell designed for one. I remember we
hauled our meagre furnishings in front of the door so that it
could not open and barricaded it also with ourselves. When
the Governor came along with the warder and we still
refused to budge we heard the prisoner outside shout 'Take
cover, girls!' – only just had time to drop to the floor before
a bullet came right through the spyhole and lodged in the
opposite wall. After firing the Governor said 'I hope there
will be four dead bodies there in the morning' – that's how

much they thought of us. But we still wouldn't open the door. This state of affairs went on for a few days but then as one of our number grew poorly, we had to relent. I was already ten months in that hell-hole with no trial, thanks to Finney, so I decided I had to join some of the other women on hunger strike because there was nothing left to me any more, nothing left to me but me.

ALICE. Nell was twenty-one days on strike before they released her.
I was almost out of my mind.
I had PJ walk Dublin and Meath trying to get some succour from old comrades now working with the Government and I assailed every contact of my own, eventually...
thankfully... she was put out.

NELL. Into the January dawn of another bloody year.

PJ. You'd hardly have known Nell Farrell that spring of '23. So wizened and frail and with just a grey scrape left of her once lustrous dark hair. She looked more like Alice's grandmother than her sister when we took her home to Kells. Mountjoy had stripped her of all her vigour, all her bloom.

ALICE. Yet she never doubted the cause of the Irish Republic as I might. The cause. The fight. It was written so deep into her heart. A broken hope cradling in the muscle of her, frothing and fizzing constantly in her brain.

NELL. We can't let them steal it from us, Alice, our Republic. We can't let them stack it full of businessmen, landlords, piety and priests. They will leave us nothing!

PJ. I loved Nell but I was nervous enough of having her back under our roof, she was down but not out if I knew her at all and with Alice's nursing I knew she'd soon be back on form. I just prayed that the blasted split might finish. That the renegades might come to heel before she was back on her feet because I was just beginning to get a bit of business going with the printing and Alice was fluttering again with a new little one due in the June.

ALICE. Another baby stirring.
Another life beating within me. And I was happy to have the

little mite but wanted to imagine a life of real freedom for her. A life of education, opportunity and promise. I wanted to believe like Nell believed.
Nell...

What's this?

NELL. What's what?

ALICE. What are you doing out here in the printing sheds?

NELL. I'm just... just printing off a few leaflets...

ALICE. A few?... There's hundreds!
O my God, Nell, when did you start this?

NELL. Start what?

ALICE. Unbelievable, you are just unbelievable. I should have known...
sitting out here with PJ and pretending to be interested in how to set up the letters... how to set up the press...

NELL. I AM interested!

ALICE. 'Well now, PJ, isn't that just mighty...
Well now, PJ, aren't you some man!'

NELL *laughs*.

Do you think he won't know?!

NELL. He hasn't said anything yet...

ALICE. Jesus help us if he sees these...
(*Reading*.) 'Every West Briton in Ireland supports the Treaty, now why is that?'

NELL. Do you like the colour?

ALICE. It's not the colour that will get you arrested... get us all bloody arrested!

NELL. Sure you have nothing to do with it.
You've thrown in your lot with the Staters.

ALICE. How can you say that?
How can you possibly say that, Nell, after everything?

NELL. Well you've been fierce quiet down here.

ALICE. Quiet?!
I've been tending to my sister in case you didn't notice!
I've only been nursing her back to life...

NELL. Well then. Congratulations! You did a great job.
They are not all bet in Meath you know, there's still the few like Swan willing to take a shot and the women are up for anything...

ALICE. What women?

NELL. The Cumann in Navan.
They're helping distribute the leaflets.

ALICE. Unbelievable.

NELL. Come on, Alice. Join us. You've always been far better than me with words and I was thinking we could have a new bulletin, a WAR bulletin informing the good people of Ireland of all the new atrocities being committed by their own army!

ALICE. But this is different.

NELL. How is it different?

ALICE. The enemy is our own people.

NELL. Exactly. Betrayed by our own people.

ALICE. I don't think I have the stomach for it.

NELL. Well you either believe in the Irish Republic or you don't.
I believe.
You can make your own decision.

PJ. And so it began again.

ALICE. It all began again.

PJ. And with it came our end.

ALICE. I loved love PJ with all my heart, and James and the new bounce of life inside always took precedence over any work or politics or distraction... but I found that I could just as easy keep house while giving a few hours to Nell and the Republic.

NELL. It was like old times.

ALICE. Old times. And I realised that I had missed it all so much! The sense of purpose, the comradery, the variety of tasks. I was back in my element. Back with Nell by my side.

NELL. We were not only designing and printing the new pamphlets but also got ourselves a few tins of paints and met up with the ladies from Navan to plaster '*Up the Republic*' on the gable end of a few sheds and a house on the Market Square.

ALICE. There was hell-to-pay from the local barracks when the women fired stones and eggs at the young cadets sent out to wash it away.

NELL. I'd like to think that our campaign caused a bit of a stir in the population of Meath but I know for sure that it was greatly appreciated in Dublin. We could print buckets of material on PJ's print blocks and soon established a grand little line of distribution from Kells to the North and from Dunboyne to the South.

PJ. I knew well what the girls were at but turned my head the other way because there was so much disharmony in the country I couldn't face bringing it into the sanctity of my home.
Home.
Jamesie rolling and kicking and starting to crawl around the house. A right bonny little man and no wonder because he never stopped guzzling at his mother. And Alice. O Jesus, Alice, with her smile and her keen eyes. I can still picture her. Picture it all as she leans down over the kettle, only knee-high to a grass-hopper but perfectly formed... perfect... the heat of her face, the curl of her hair, the strong sweet smell of her, Jesus, I can't bear it, I can't bear to remember...

ALICE. I tried to keep my hands down.
I tried to keep my arms around my belly.
I begged... I...

All was wild again.

PJ. All was war again.

NELL. All was action.

PJ. I don't know if it was the egg incident at the barracks in
Navan or the cumulative effect of their efforts but the girls
came to the attention of the Staters in Dublin.

NELL. Who called upon their Free State Captain in Kells to call
out and put some manners on us.

PJ. The Captain called right enough and took to warning me
that if Nell and Alice didn't stop with their nefarious
activities he'd be forced to take action. It was an odd
encounter. We knew each other all our lives. I said I'd have a
word with the girls but sure... I knew they couldn't be
stopped.

ALICE. We couldn't be stopped.

PJ. Please don't take me for a fool, Alice.

ALICE. I don't. I'm sorry. I just didn't want to get you
involved.
I know how you feel about the Treaty...

PJ. The Treaty is a bloody disaster.
The only winners as far as I can see are the British and they
must be loving this! They must be just loving to watch us
slaughter each other, doesn't it play rightly into their notion
of who we are!
'The fighting Irish.'
'Unruly Irish.'
'Thick fucking Irish.' That thick that we would throw it all
away, our one real chance at independence...

ALICE. But that's just it... they think it's theirs to give.
Well it isn't, our independence is ours to fight for.

PJ. O, Alice...

ALICE. They think they still own us with their bloody oath and
their empire and their sickening bloody benevolence...

PJ. It's dangerous what you're doing.
This is dangerous...

ALICE. Hasn't it always been dangerous?... I thought we
crossed that line years ago...

PJ. But what about James?
And what about the little one you have inside of you?

ALICE. Sure isn't it them that I'm fighting for.
They deserve their Republic, our Republic, PJ.
What happened to you, you said we'd never have to give
up...

PJ. I won't go to war with my own countrymen.
I won't kill my own neighbours. I won't.
No Republic is worth that.

ALICE. Right so.
I hear you.
I respect you.
But I think different.
You've got to leave me at it, PJ.

PJ. I'm afraid for you, Alice.

ALICE. Don't be, PJ.
Please don't ever be afraid.

PJ. But I was afraid.
Afraid for Alice. Afraid for Ireland... because this fight, this
war, this civil war was different... this civil war was hell...
a war without mercy... a war without love... a tired, dirty,
savage war that turned us in on ourselves... that corrupted
us all.

NELL. The boys in Dublin must have decided it was time to
shut us down. So who decided to come down and stop us at
the printing only **Finney**.

PJ. **Finney.**

ALICE. **Finney.**

NELL. I heard he still had a head on him that I'd been let out of
Mountjoy.

PJ. They came.
He came.
In the dead of night.

NELL. Finney.

PJ. And they came.
He came.
With murder on his mind...

ALICE. There were at least six of them burst into the house
with torches and rifles and boots...

PJ. Kicking down the door.

NELL. It was clear that Finney was set to terrorise...

PJ (*as Finney*). 'Well, well, Nell so this is where you washed up?'

NELL. Fuck off, Finney, you've no business here.
This is me sister's house and she's not involved.

PJ (*as Finney. He laughs*). 'Do you take me for a fool? Sure
we've known for months that it was the two of you behind
all them seditious little leaflets littering the fine towns of
Meath and beyond...'

ALICE. You know nothing of the sort.
This is my husband's business...

PJ. It is, it's my business.

ALICE. My husband who served in the same army you do...

NELL. Before you betrayed us all and set about murdering your
own comrades... and comrades that saved your miserable
hide countless times from the British.

PJ (*as Finney*). 'Ah Nell, Nell, Nell will you never learn?'

ALICE. And with that he punched her full-force in the face.
PJ leapt forward –

PJ. But two of Finney's minions were set on me...

(*As Finney.*) 'PJ Reilly, I remember you.
Pump House, wasn't it?
Well, how the mighty have fallen.
I can't say I'm keen on the company you're keeping so
I think we might ask you to just sit this one out in another
room.'

ALICE. And poor PJ was hauled through kicks and punches and locked into the back kitchen.

PJ (*as Finney*). 'Just you and me now, girls, and a little matter of a printing press.'

NELL. Finney was a strong bastard, he could drag the two of us out to the shed while his boys poked their rifles into us. Then he ordered them to smash up the blocks.

ALICE. That's our livelihood your hoodlums are destroying!

PJ (*as Finney*). 'Well now you should have thought of that before you threw your lot in with the sister here... now I'll have to make sure you're good and sorry. Give me the grease here, Muldoon.'

NELL. And Finney began pouring some class of axel grease onto poor Alice, all over her hair, her back... she was screaming and I could see him start to pull at her shift. 'Leave her, leave her for the love of God, can't you see that she's well on in her pregnancy.'

ALICE. Don't hurt me please.

NELL. But Finney had no love of God, no love of anyone but himself and he was excited now, delighted, I could see it in the torchlight, in the twist of his face. 'Lord she's only lovely, Nell, your sister.' I pleaded, pleaded with to the other men to stop him, stop it... but the more I pleaded, the more he seemed to enjoy himself and they just stood on aghast.

ALICE. Finney threw me smack back against the wall of the printing shed.

NELL. I screamed and scraped and bit at the hands that were now all over me... I got free and leapt onto Finney's back but they tore me off and started to whip me on his orders with their Sam Brown belts. Then one of them began to pour the same grease all over me.

ALICE. I tried to keep my hands down.
I tried to keep my arms around my belly.
I begged... I begged for my baby...
'Please please please don't hurt me or you'll hurt her.'

NELL. But Finney didn't listen.
  Finney held Alice by the hair.
  Finney pushed Alice's stricken body into the wall as he
  pumped and pumped.
  'Jesus Christ stop... stop before you kill her'... and he
  turned, laughing as he buttoned up his fly, a blow of the rifle
  butt to my jaw.

PJ (as Finney). 'That might shut you up for a while now, Nell.'

NELL. And another blow to my skull for good measure.

PJ (as Finney). 'And you can take this as a message to your
  irregular soldier friends.
  Give up or you're all FUCKED.'

NELL. And he laughed. Laughed! As he walked back out
  through the house, cool as you like and the other eejits
  staggering after him, one of them snivelling to me 'I'm sorry,
  missus, I'm sorry.'
  And then silence.

PJ. Silence.

NELL. The most awful silence.
  Alice?

PJ. It was one of the neighbours finally plucked up the courage
  to come into the house. They had heard it all. Seen the
  torches...

NELL. The neighbour found PJ tied and bound in the kitchen.
  Me unconscious in the grass.
  And Alice in a river of blood.

ALICE. It was the violence of the outrage that brought little
  Róisín on,
  she pushed as best she could to get into the world but
  something ruptured in me and I couldn't save her, couldn't
  save either of us, so my poor little girl came flowing out in a
  haemorrhage of death as we both bled away into the night.

NELL. Alice was dead.

PJ. Alice was dead.

NELL. The shock of it.

PJ. The shock…

NELL. The attack when it was reported caused horror in the little town of Kells and shock-waves throughout the whole country. Uniforms and priests and neighbours and family came with comfort no matter which side their loyalties lay.

PJ. The Free State Captain in Kells interviewed the local men who were ordered in as part of Finney's raid and they corroborated everything Nell and I attested to. They were mostly new recruits traumatised by what they had witnessed. I took their testimony to the Department of Justice up in Dublin and sat outside the Dáil for days until the head of the Free State Army agreed to see me. 'My wife worked for this country's first president', I told the newspaper men 'and now she's been murdered by a Commander under the employ of the second.'
I wanted to see Finney court-martialled.
I wanted to see Finney hanged.

NELL. But the truth of our story didn't suit the teetering new Irish Government.

PJ. And the truth of our story didn't suit the new army of the Irish Free State.

NELL. The actions of Ireland's soldiers had to be seen to be beyond reproach. And the actions of Ireland's Commanders had to be seen to be justified, beatified, blessed by God himself.
And so it began again.

ALICE. It began again.

PJ. Our end.

NELL. 'Patrick Finney is a national army commander with an established record.'

PJ. 'Patrick Finney is a married man with six children.'

NELL. 'Patrick Finney is a true patriot who has devoted himself to the safe establishment of an Independent Ireland.'

PJ. 'Patrick Finney wasn't the one who committed the outrage.'

NELL. 'It was Patrick Finney that called them off.'

PJ. 'Patrick Finney wasn't there…'

ALICE. You could see the lie take hold, take hold like a creeping contagion snaking through the countryside. A blight rolling in on the mist… .

PJ. 'Sure that Nell Farrell was always trouble.'

ALICE. 'A firebrand. A hothead. A diehard.'

NELL. 'And the sister was no better, codded poor Reilly up to the two eyes they did. Did you know he was a cuckold?! Did you know the child wasn't even his…'

PJ. By the time the Free State Propaganda machine was finished with Alice and Nell they were running a brothel out there in the print sheds and worshipping the devil in their spare time…

ALICE. All sympathy switched to *Finney*.

NELL. *Dangerous, treacherous women trying to smear a good man's name.*

PJ. The neighbours, the soldiers, old comrades, they knew the truth all right and they couldn't look me in the eye but they closed ranks all the same, closed ranks around their new Irish Free State.

ALICE. *Finney* never got court-martialled.

NELL. *Finney* never lost his command.

PJ. The Irish Free State Army maintained an immaculate record.

ALICE. War makes heroes and demons doesn't it?

PJ. So how could war in Ireland be any different?

NELL. No matter what the priests say.
Or the Staters.
Or the books.

ALICE. It was less than two months after that night that a truce was called.

NELL. Another truce.

PJ. Not that it meant anything to me.

NELL. The Anti-Treaty forces put down their guns.

ALICE. It was all to be sorted through politics now.

PJ. Politics? Politics?
As if we hadn't had our fill of politics.
As if the country hadn't been beaten, blasted, blown apart for politics... and for years... for all those years... all those dreams... all those men... women... gone... and for what? For what?
What did Alice die for?

Why did Alice die, Nell... tell me that?
Why did you ever come back here?
Why did you always have to keep it up?
Could you not have just accepted the Treaty like the rest of us and let the country get on with building your bloody Republic?
She's gone.
Alice is gone.
My Alice.
And there's nothing you or anyone else can do to bring her back.

NELL. All was recrimination now.
All was guilt.
All was blame.

PJ. Life became impossible.

NELL. PJ's entire family were subject to a boycott unless they agreed that Finney was innocent.

PJ. My own brother told me I had to stop bothering the soldiers and the new police force in looking for justice for Alice, I had to stop insisting that 'something happened' that night.

(*As brother.*) 'We all have to move on.'

ALICE. Said PJ's brother.

PJ (*as brother*). 'There's been enough of anarchy.
Enough of destruction.
We all just want a bit of peace.'

ALICE. Where do you put that?
    Where do you put such a lie?

PJ. Deep into the heart of you, Alice, until it festers and rots.
    Until it devours you from the inside out.

NELL. PJ began to disappear into himself.
    He couldn't even sit with his son.

PJ. The child reminded me too much of Alice, of my impotency,
    my failure to save her on that night...

NELL. It was like he was slowly sinking.
    He couldn't care for the boy.

ALICE. My boy.

NELL. Could barely get himself up and dressed in the mornings
    so I thought I better stay on in Alice's house in the hope that
    he might rally...

ALICE. But then the priest arrived.

PJ. The priest.

NELL. The slick young curate with his message straight from
    God.

PJ (*as priest*). 'You can't be living under the one roof when
    you're not blood relatives. It's not right. It's a bad
    example...'

    What?
    What on earth are you saying?

ALICE. And he had the perfect fix of course.

PJ (*as priest*). 'I understand that you need a woman to look after
    the infant, PJ, so myself and the parish priest have decided
    you might get married yourselves so as to preserve decency.'

NELL. Decency! Decency, is it?

ALICE. Nell saw red.

NELL. I saw red.
    And you think the decent thing to do is to marry my sister's
    husband! And after the bastards you drop communion into

every Sunday shamed her, raped her, murdered her and her child! You limp little fucker, you can take your pasty face and your rosary right out of here before I blow your bloody head off...

ALICE. And Nell shoved her little old Wesson up into his oversized nose.
And PJ laughed.

PJ. I did.
I laughed.

ALICE. The first time I heard him laugh since... since the outrage, since that night.
Because I never left his side.

NELL. No, she never left his side.

ALICE. How could I?
I just slipped deep deep into the heart of him.

PJ. Deep down into the core of my soul.

ALICE. Until we could be together again.
Me and PJ and our little one.

NELL. And I thought, I hoped, I believed there might have been just a morsel of forgiveness in that laugh... a morsel of love... another truce perhaps?

PJ. Well you certainly sent him scarpering, Nell.

He laughs.

NELL (*laughing too*). I did, didn't I!
The nerve of him.
The fucking nerve...

PJ. But I knew there'd be trouble.

NELL. We knew there'd be trouble.

PJ. And sure enough the following Sunday I got the visit.

NELL. He was out cutting turf on Girley Bog –

PJ. – when I saw the Captain, two priests and the young curate come flapping over the rivets like vultures.

(*As priest.*) 'Dear God, PJ, we can't be having it. That Nell
has the whole town talking, the whole town terrorised. The
woman has lost her wits. She needs help. A spell in the local
psychiatric perhaps, to calm her down. She's no good, PJ. No
good. Pure trouble but sure you know that. No all we need
you to do now is to sign here.'

PJ. Four of them standing round me.

ALICE. Standing round him.

PJ. With the pen and all.
Sure what could I do?

ALICE. What could he do?

PJ. They'd have taken the child and all if I didn't agree.

NELL. PJ came in through the door that day like a hurricane.

PJ. Pack your bags, Nell.
Pack them fast.
I've the brother's car outside, we have to get you to Dublin,
we have to get you the hell out.

NELL. And he motored me and little Jamesie up to our old
friend, Mrs Woods, giving me everything, everything he had
left of value in this world.

PJ. You have to take him with you, Nell. Please.
Take him to hell out of this country because Ireland will only
kill him, kill the joy of him like it killed Alice.

NELL. And then he was gone, PJ.
Gone back to the ruin of his home.
The ruin of his life.

PJ. What else could I do?
I couldn't bear the world any more.
Couldn't bear the country.
So I just shut my door on it.
Shut my door.

ALICE. And faded away.

NELL. Mrs Woods had a niece, a teacher, out in Chicago so she
sent me off with a letter of introduction and Millie, the niece,

was only delighted with the company. She even got me a job
in one of the new telephone exchanges, citing technical
abilities I had apparently picked up at home. Who knew that
assembling guns and bomb-making might qualify one to be a
telephone operator? Millie was just gas. And Millie had a
grand little house on Touhy Street. And the three of us kind
of settled in to a life, me and Millie and Alice's boy.
And I found a new way to love.
A new way to be.
We raised James together in the sunshine of that city but then
one day… one day I saw a poster flickering in the breeze,
hanging off a display stand for the old Irish hall.

PJ. 'Special Guest of the Irish/American Hibernian Order
speaks tonight. 8 p.m. Patrick Finney. Patriot. Senator.
Member of the old IRA.'

NELL. My blood ran cold.

PJ. Her blood ran cold.

ALICE. Nell's blood ran cold.

NELL. The fucker was on a *talking tour*, was he?

PJ. Exploiting old exploits.
Masquerading as hero.

ALICE. Nell sat at the back of the hall.

NELL. It was him all right.
Still lean and sharp but the fight had left its mark, when he
took the stand to spill his shtick he had to lean on a cane.

ALICE. There was rheumatism in the old bones.

NELL. I could see that his speed and strength were gone.

ALICE. Nell watched him move back to the dressing rooms
after the talk surrounded by an entourage. Then she watched
the sycophants leave to prepare refreshments while Mr
Finney might change into his tuxedo for the big reception.
She slipped inside.

NELL. I slipped inside.

ALICE. Finney was sitting in his drawers with his back to the
door.

NELL. The old grey head bent, as he reached for his trousers.

ALICE. Nell had lost none of her agility despite her years.

NELL. So I was on the fucker in an instant.

ALICE. Like a cat.

NELL. I stuck my revolver into the back of his neck...
'Hello, Finney.
Do you remember me at all?'
I was about to pull the trigger when Alice's whisper landed
between us. When Alice's whisper kissed my cheek.

ALICE. Have you not heard the war is over, Nell?
It's over. Go back to Millie and to my Jamesie and live your
beautiful life.

NELL. The old bastard could sense my hesitation.

PJ (*as Finney*). 'You don't have it in you, do you, Nell?'

ALICE. Over.
It has to be over.
If there is to be love and hope and equality, Nell.

NELL. 'How about I give you a sporting chance,
That's more than you gave my sister.'

PJ. And she kicked his cane across the floor

NELL. 'Just how slow are you?'

PJ. Then Nell lit a match,

NELL. I did, I lit a match, and I stuck it to the curtains,

PJ. And watched them flame.

NELL. 'Welcome to hell, Finney. Don't hurt yourself now if
you find you have to jump out that window.'
And I turned the key in the door as I left.

PJ. The old hall went up fast.

NELL. I could hear the shouts and commotion as the crowd
burst out into the open but I didn't look back.

PJ. It was like a bonfire of the vanities.
A bonfire of arrogance, privilege, greed.

ALICE. But after fire comes the rain.
After fire comes future.

PJ/NELL. Future.

ALICE. Future.

End.

A Nick Hern Book

Raging: Three Wars/Plays first published as a paperback original in Great Britain in 2022 by Nick Hern Books Limited, The Glasshouse, 49a Goldhawk Road, London W12 8QP

Three Plays/Seven Years of Warfare in Ireland copyright © 2022 Deirdre Kinahan

Deirdre Kinahan has asserted her right to be identified as the author of this work

Cover image: Leo Byrne and Publicis Dublin

Designed and typeset by Nick Hern Books, London
Printed in Great Britain by Mimeo Ltd, Huntingdon, Cambridgeshire PE29 6XX

A CIP catalogue record for this book is available from the British Library

ISBN   978 1 83904 086 3

Woodland **CARBON**
www.woodlandcarbon.co.uk
NICK HERN BOOKS
Printed on Carbon Captured paper